# Dimensional Lenses

Cary William White

Copyright © 2018 Cary William White  Wildwood Pub

All rights reserved.

ISBN:1719374155
ISBN-13:9781719374156

I wish to give thanks to all of the artists in my life. Vera, Jack Steve, Greg, Nessa, Dustin, Raquel Maldonaldo Ogle, Gilmore, D.C. Johnson, George Thomason, Cool Hand Clemens, Gordon Rowland, Michael Brown, and Estuardo Maldonaldo, Don and Susan Moser

# CONTENTS

## I. PHOTO JOURNEYS

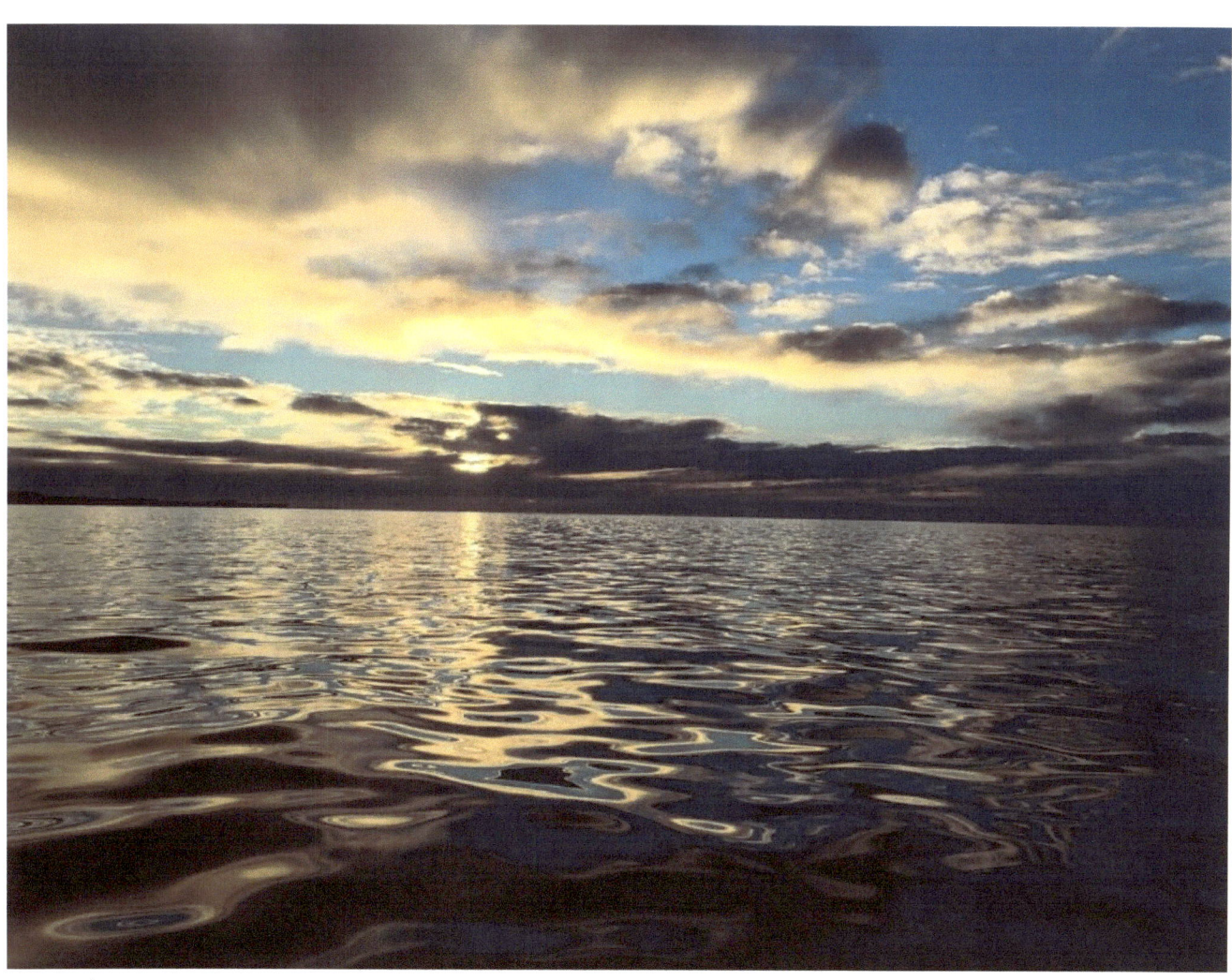

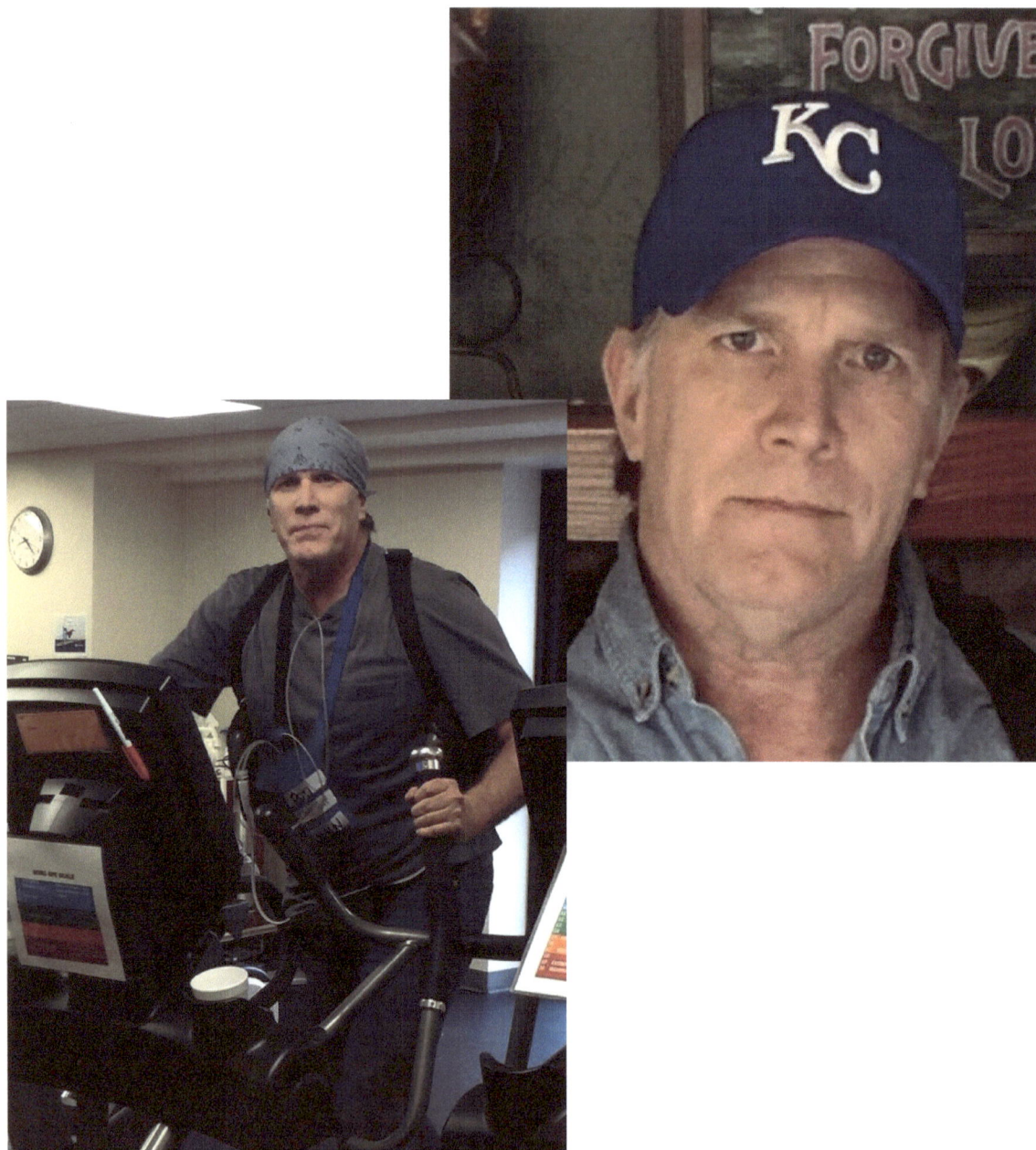

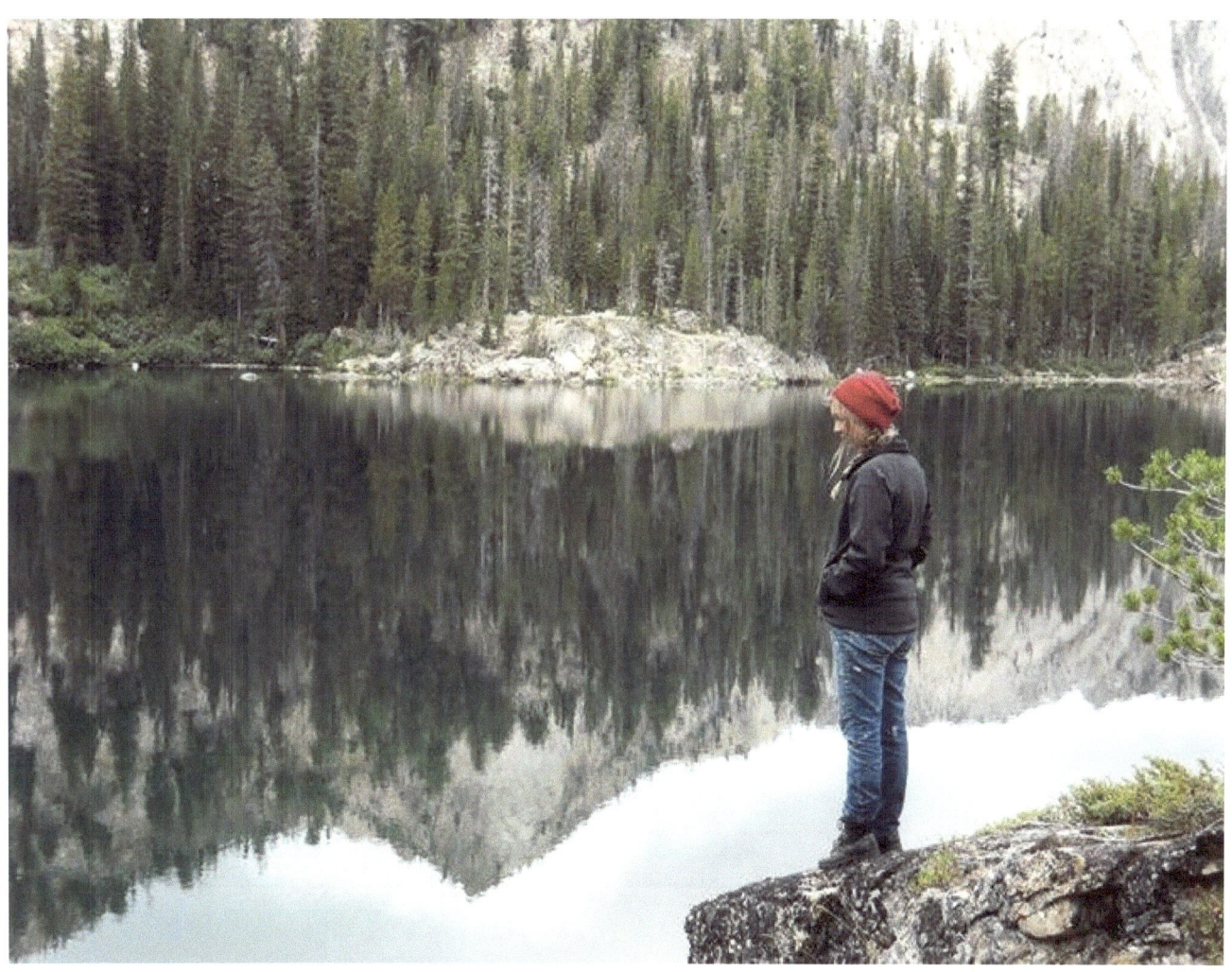

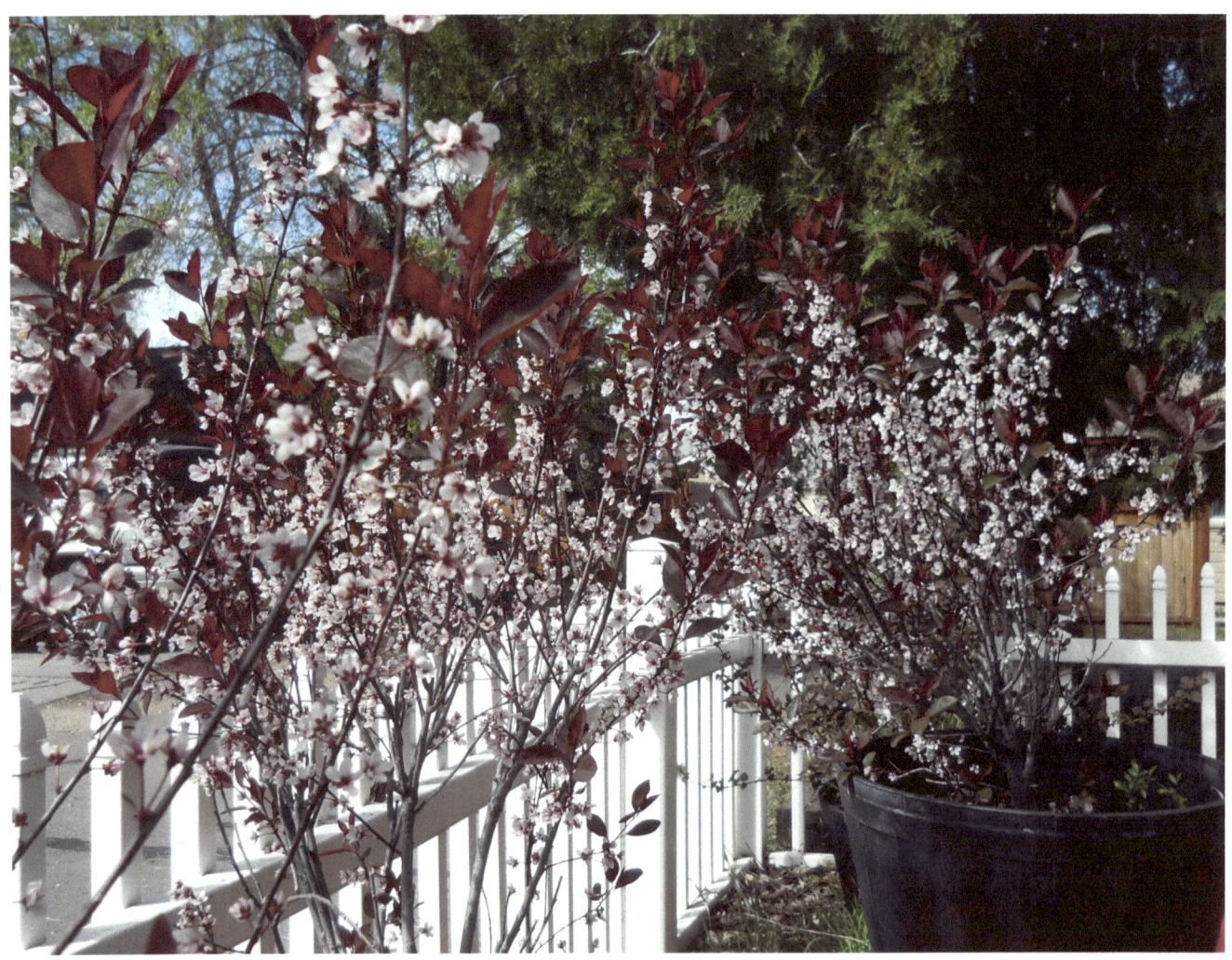

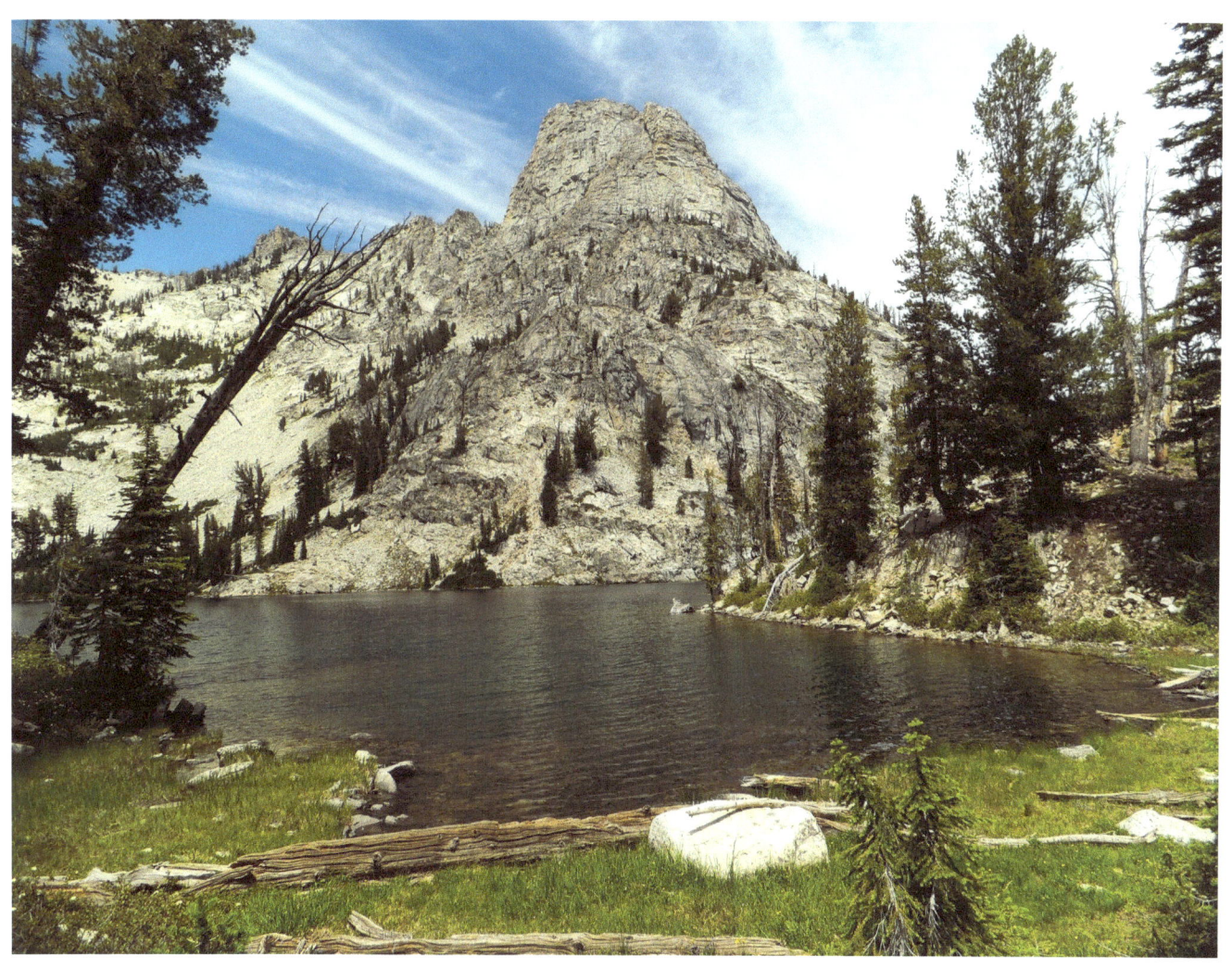

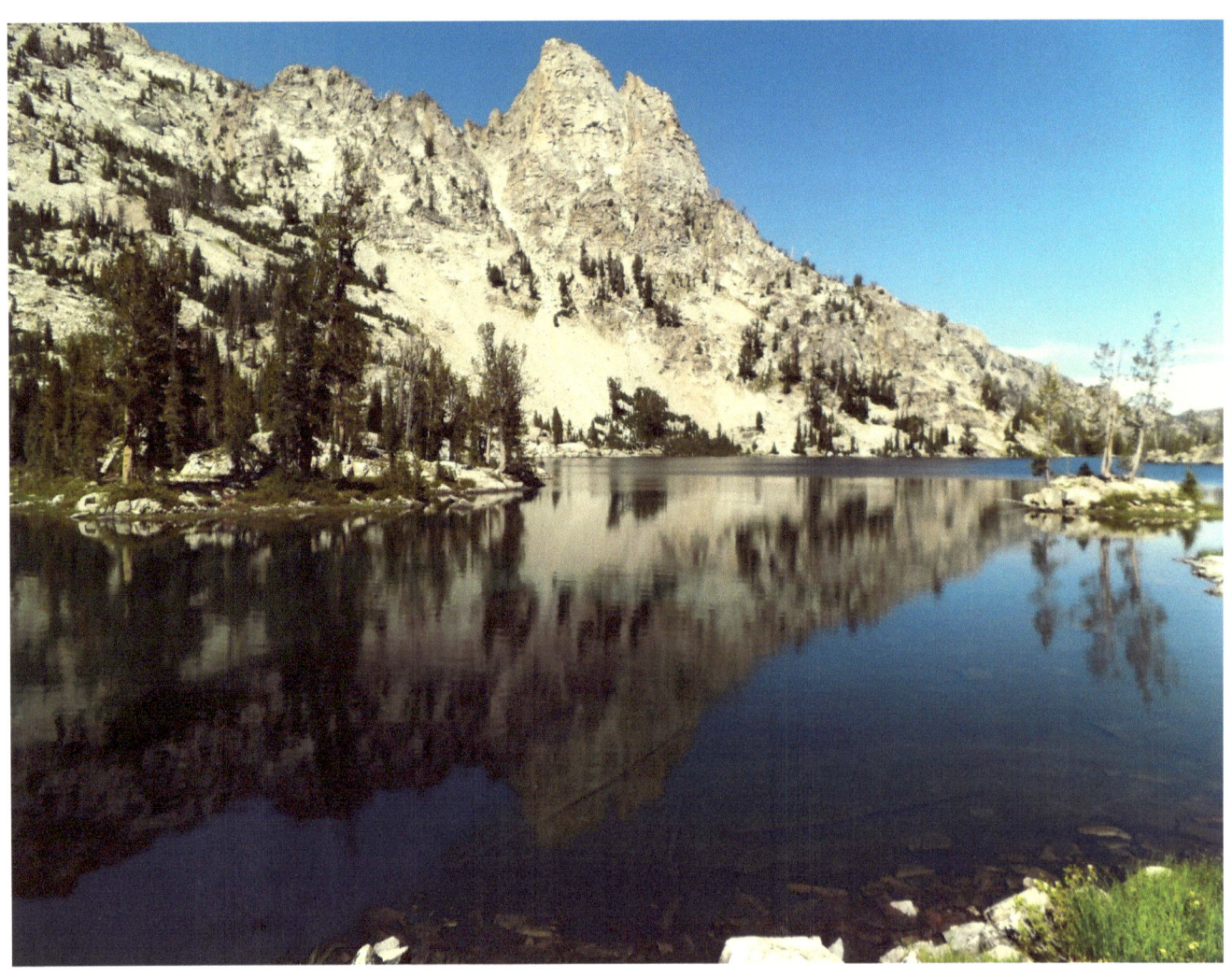

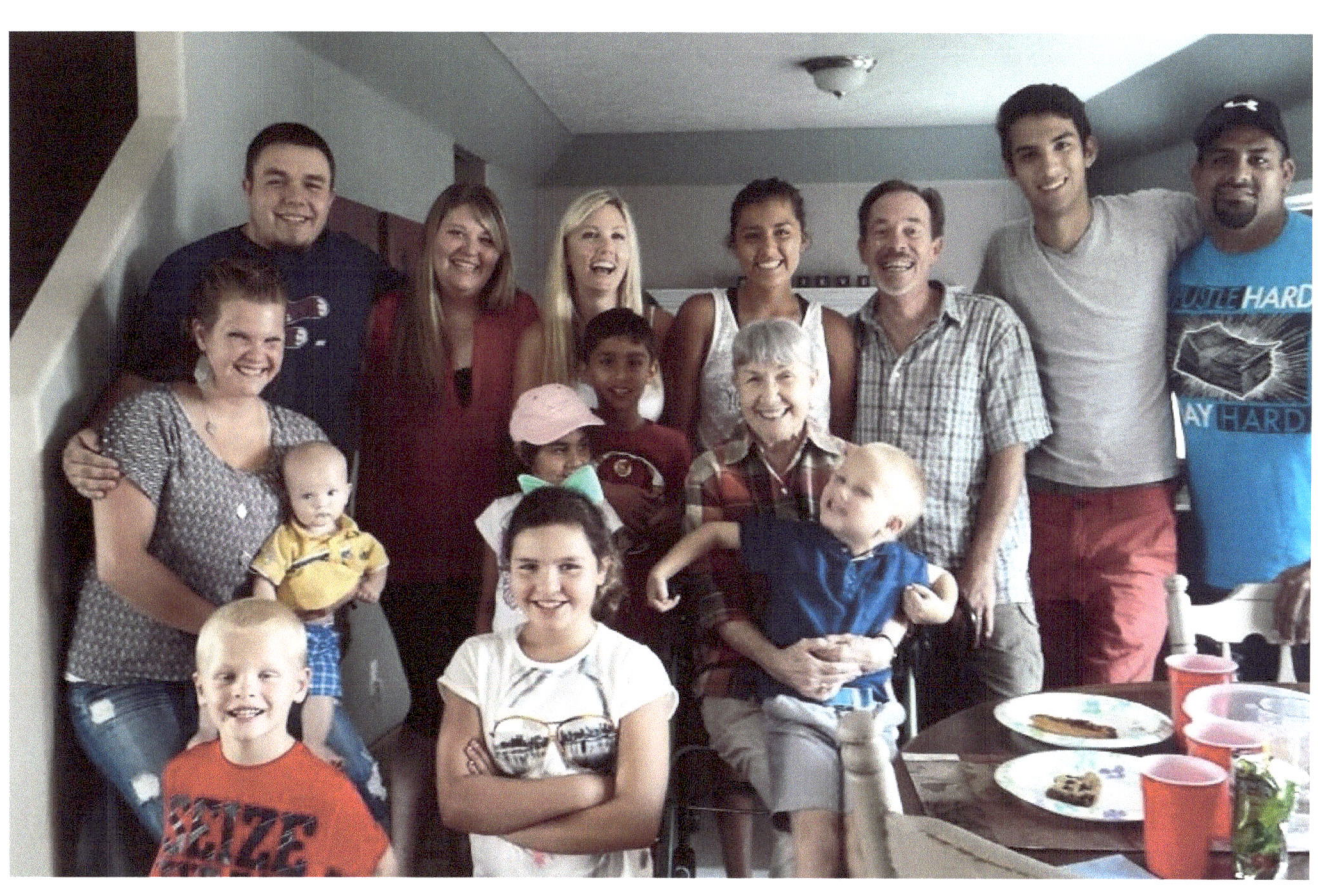

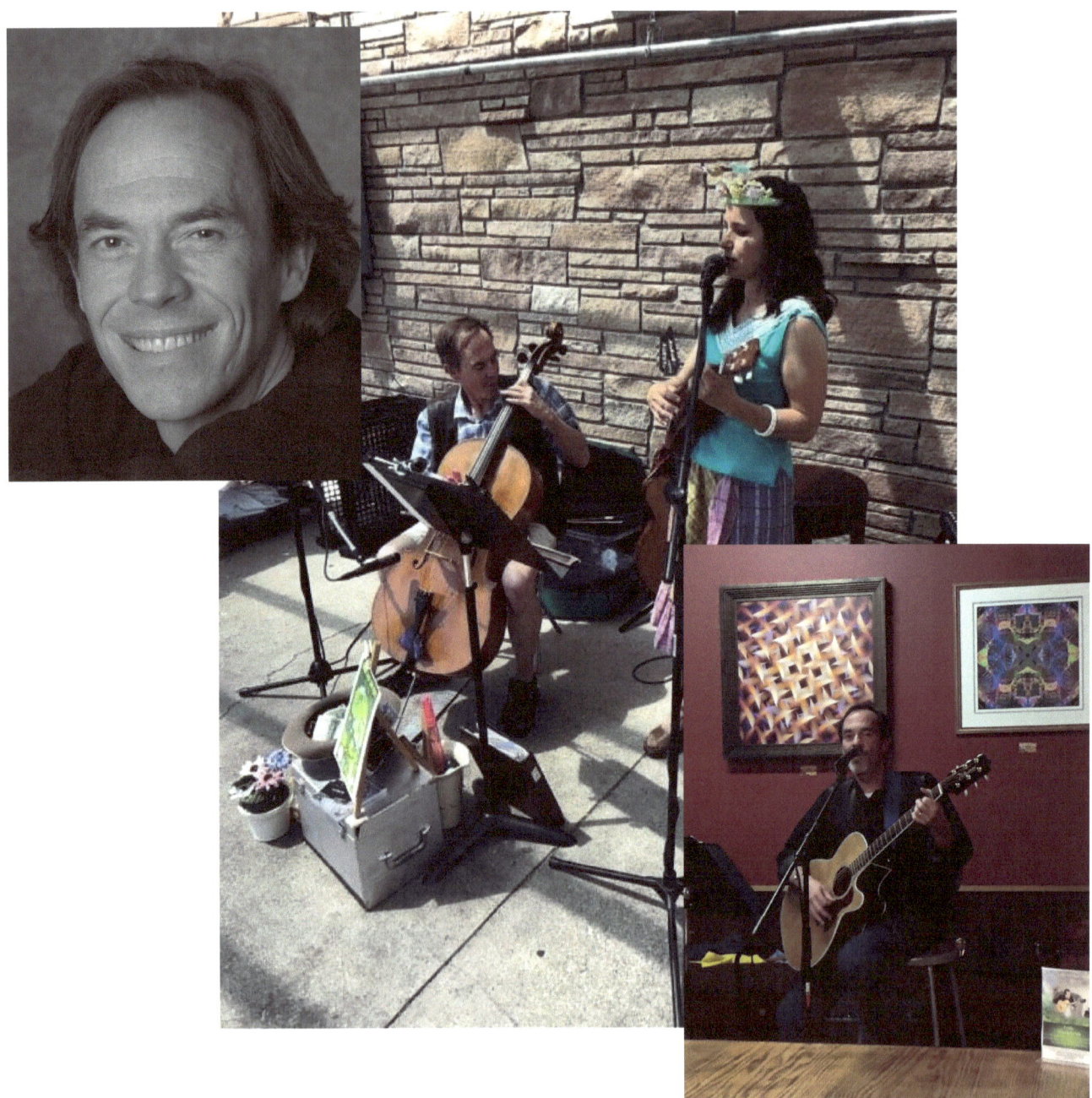

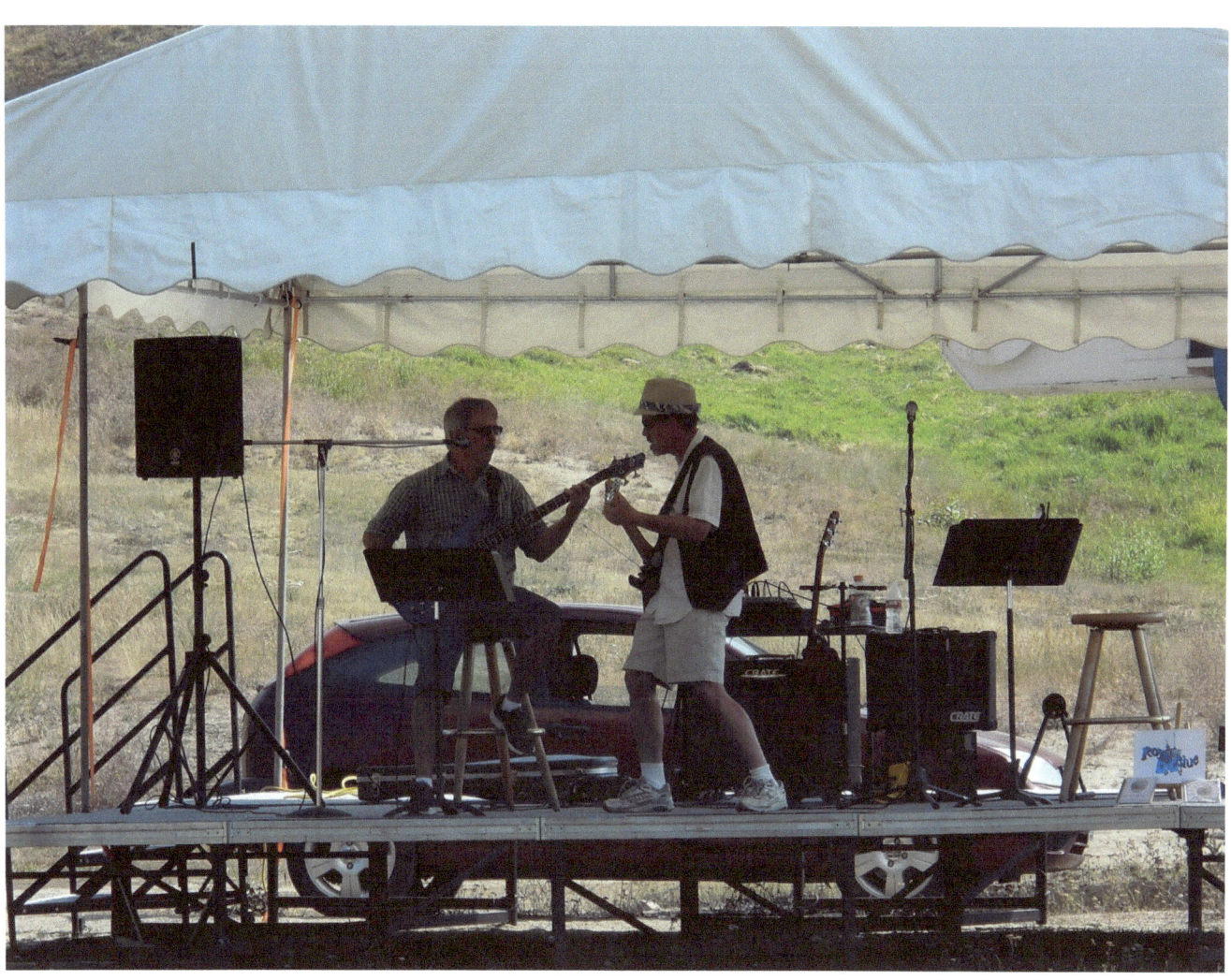

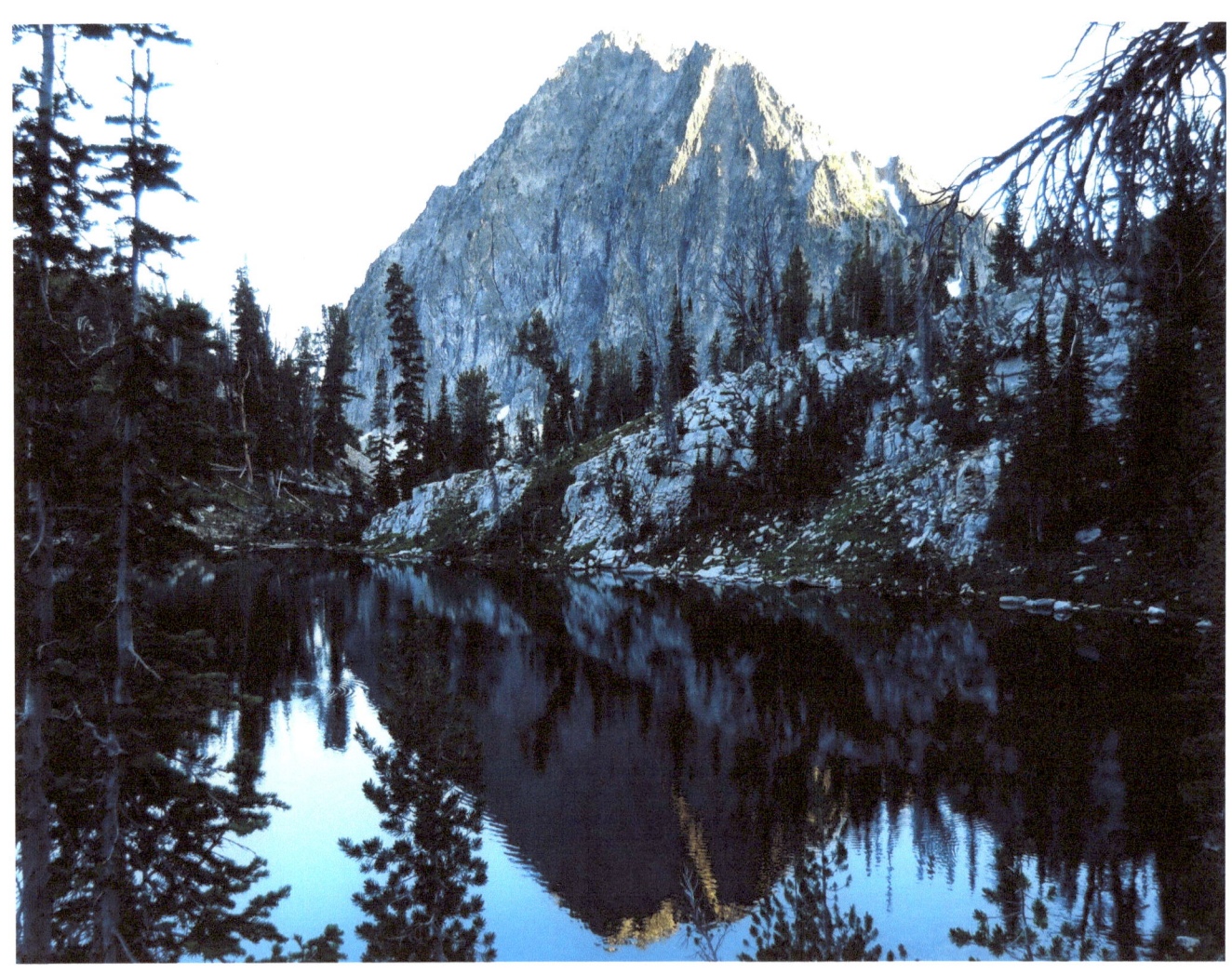

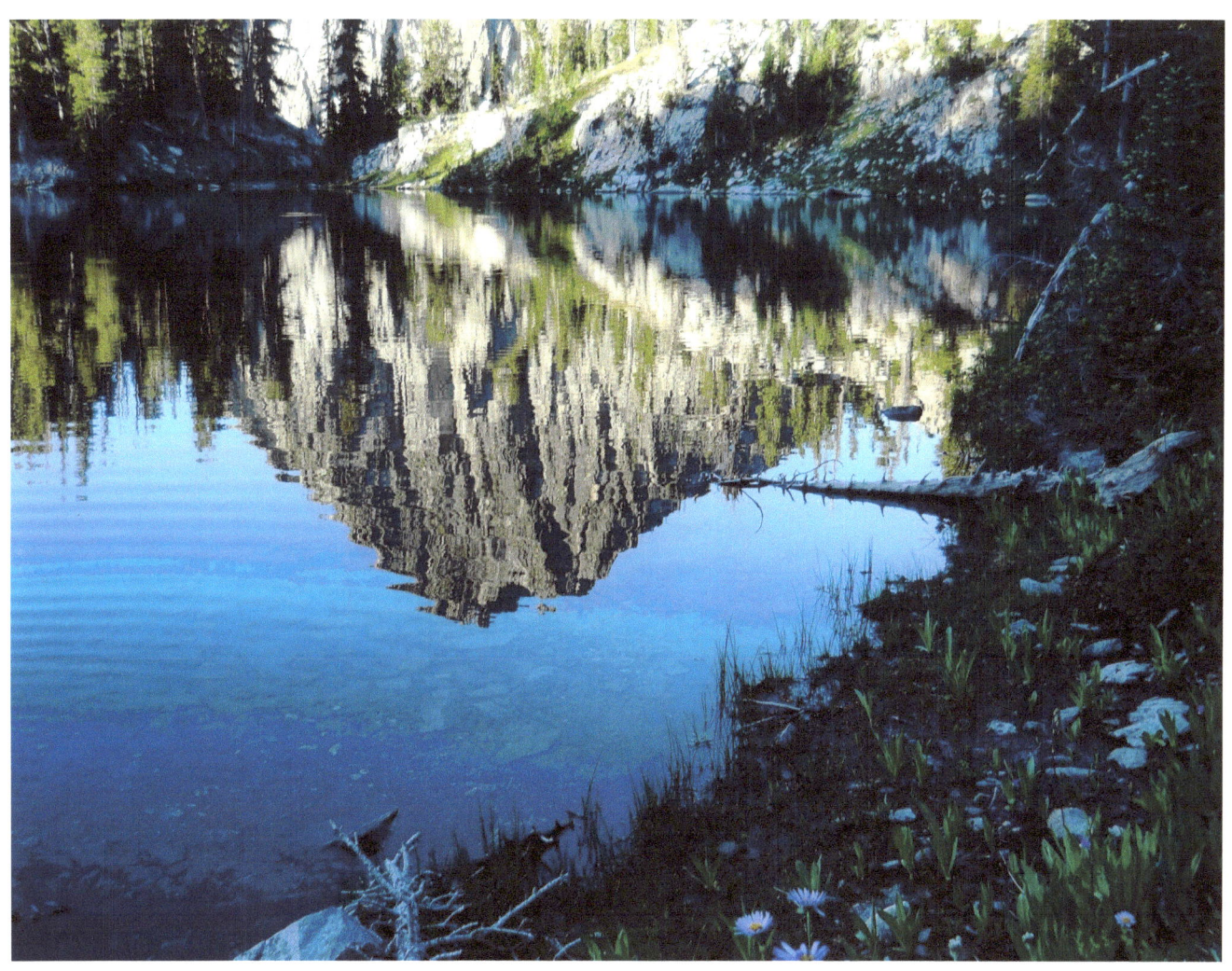

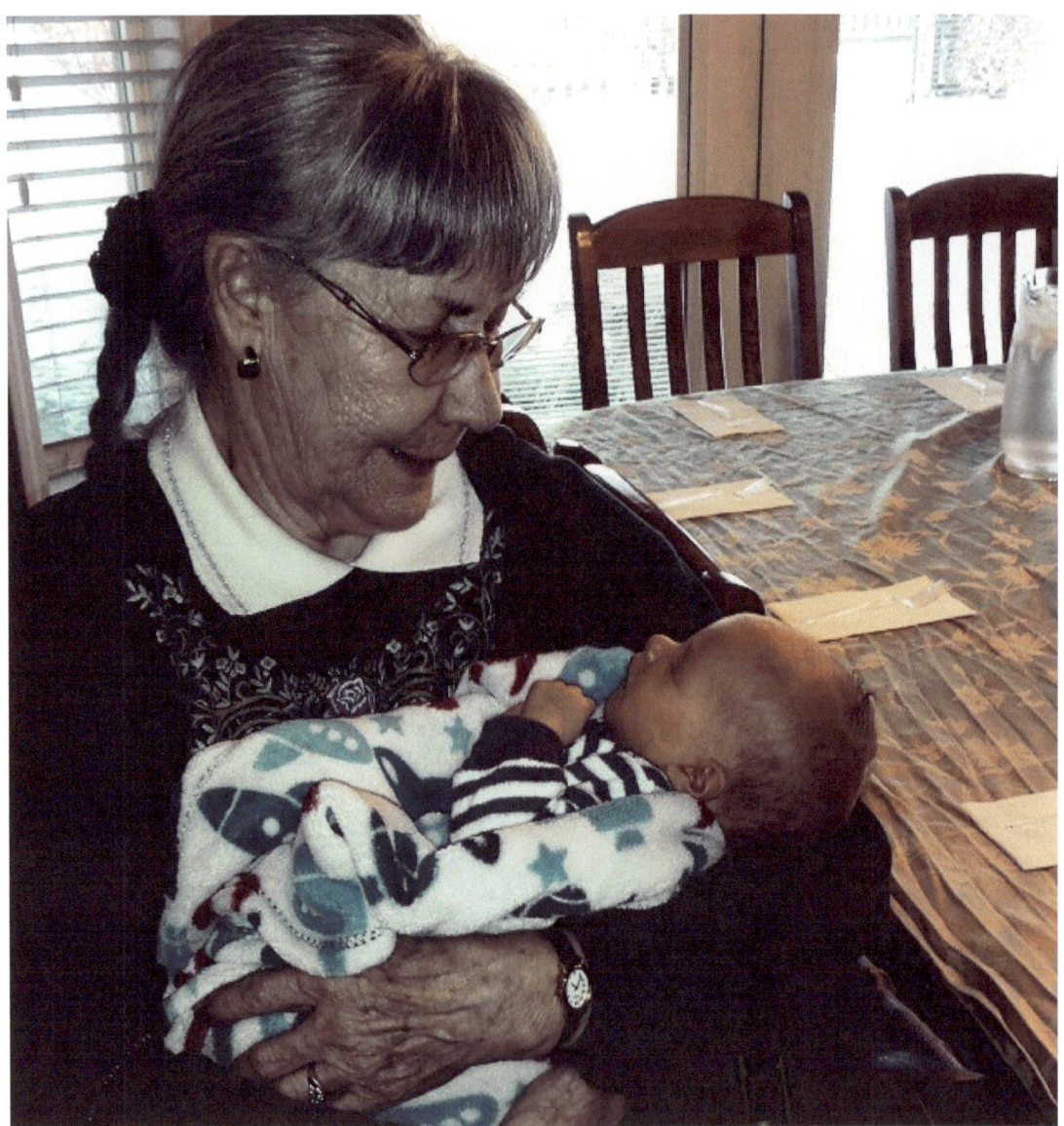

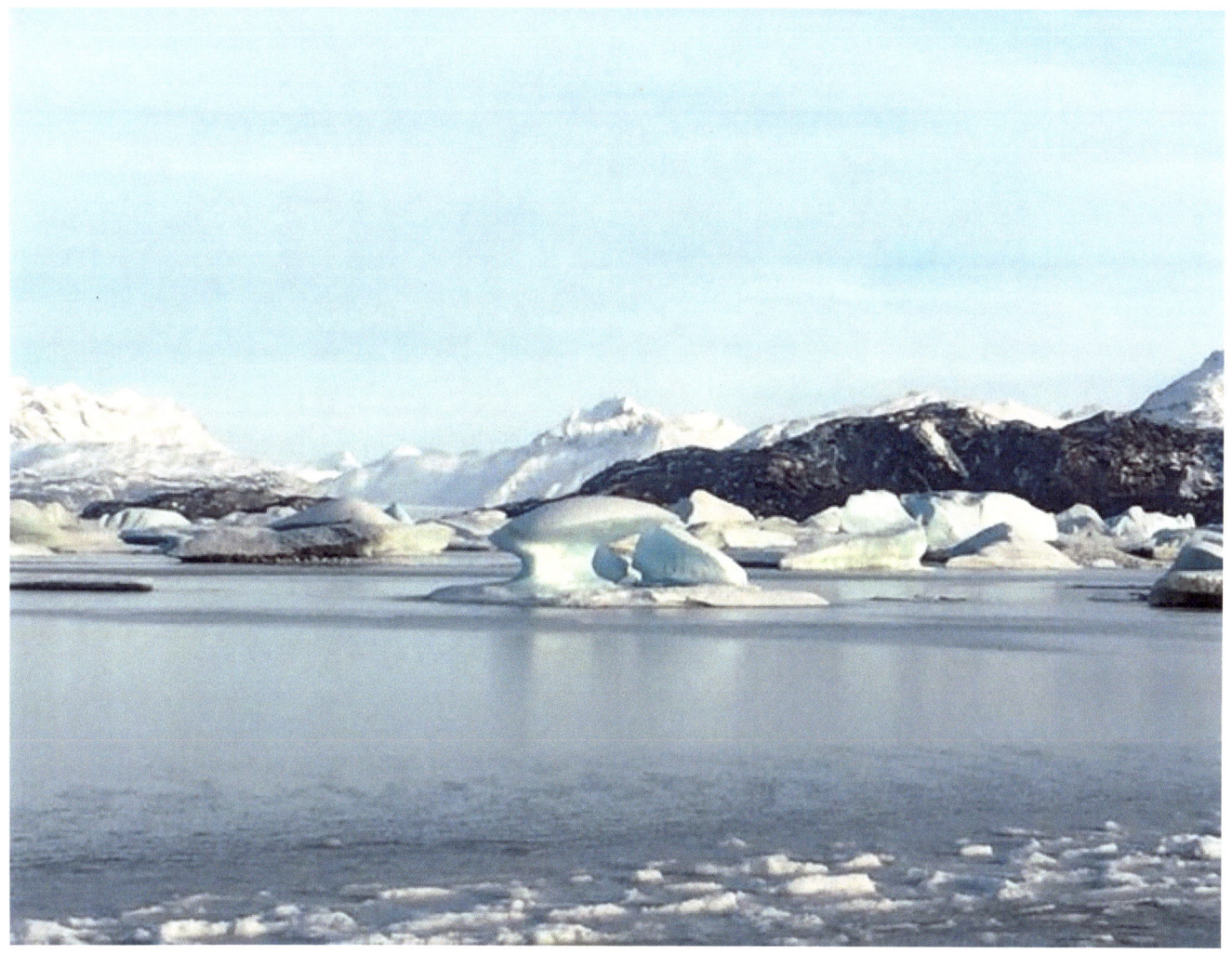

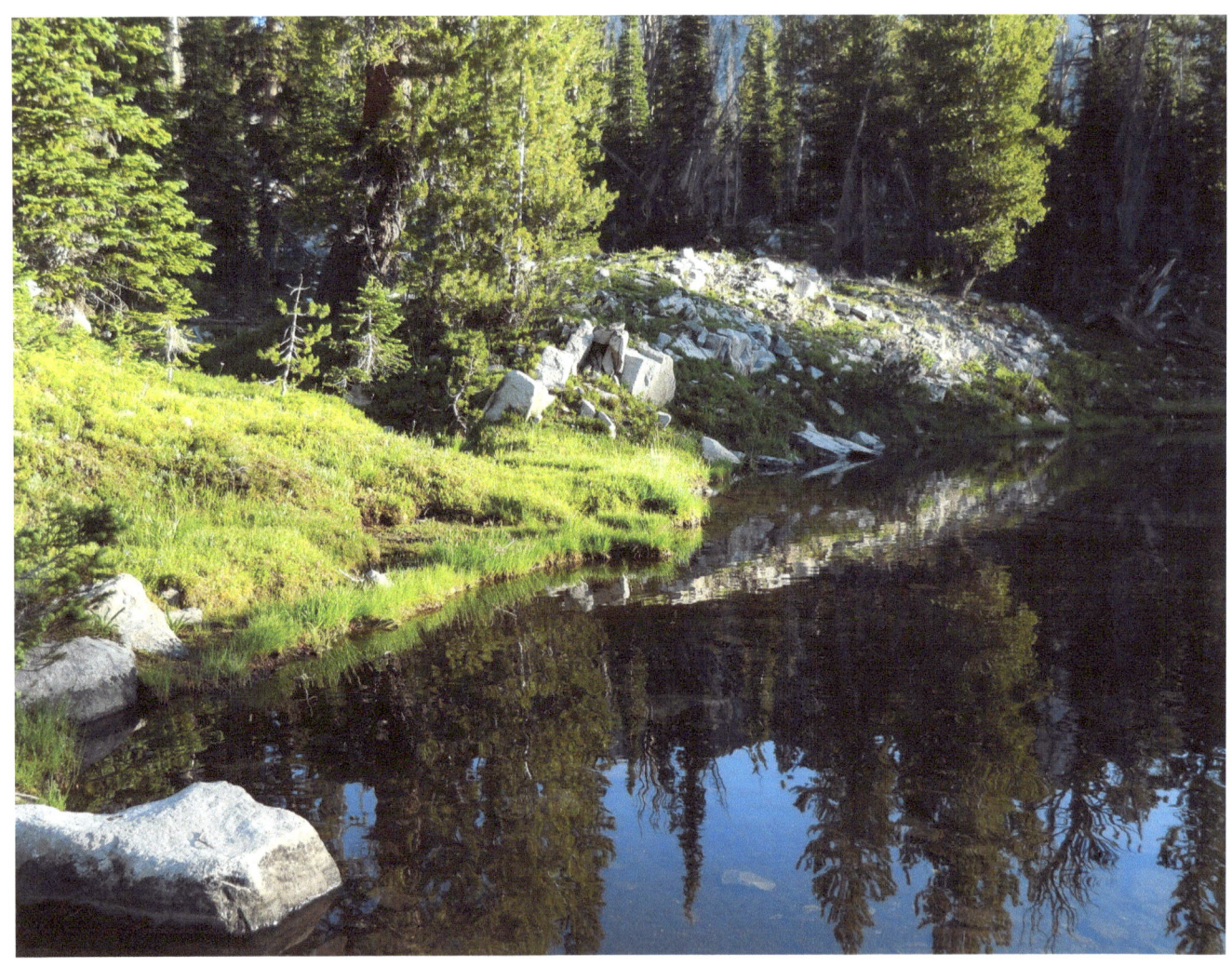

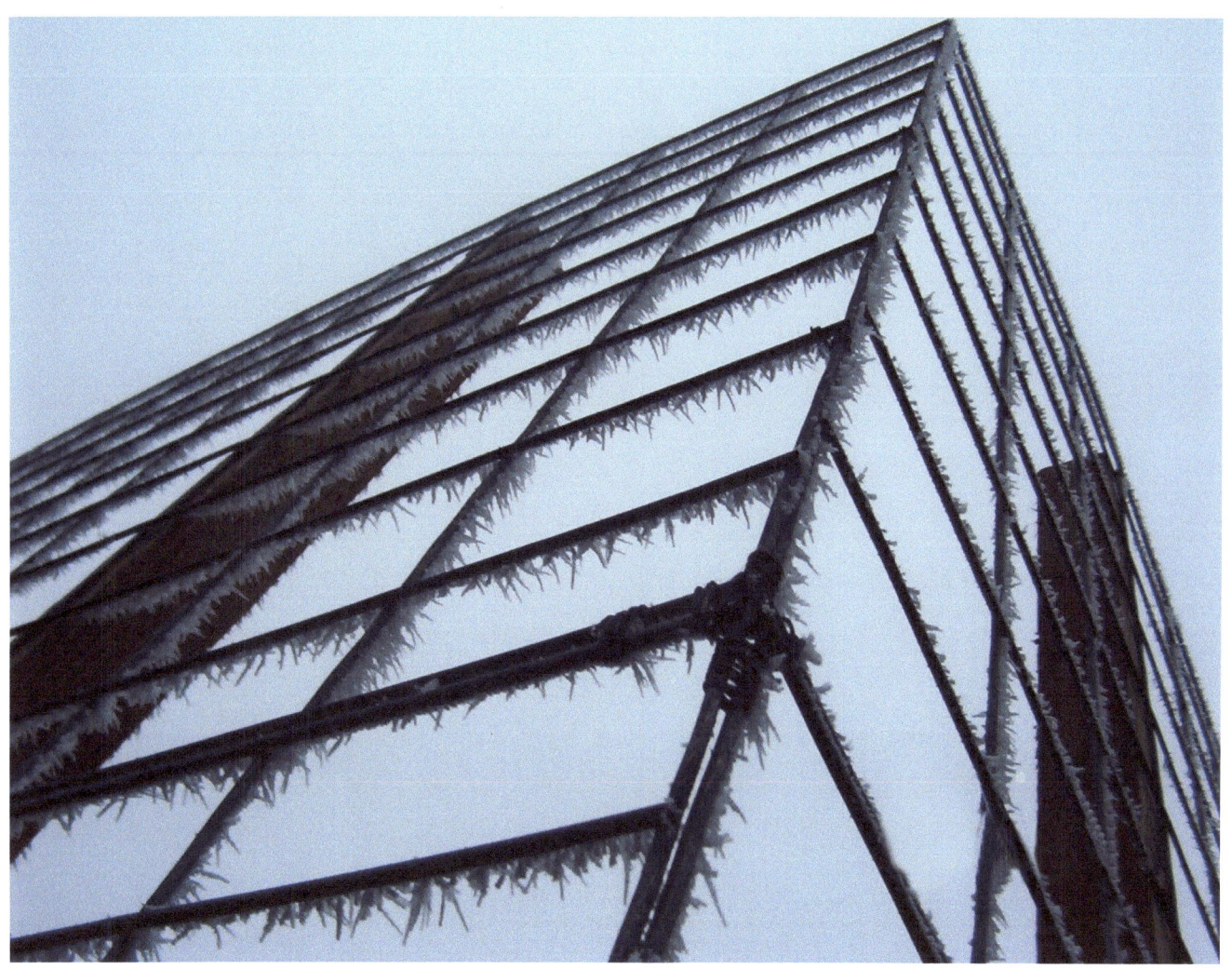

# II. WORLDS WITHIN WORLDS

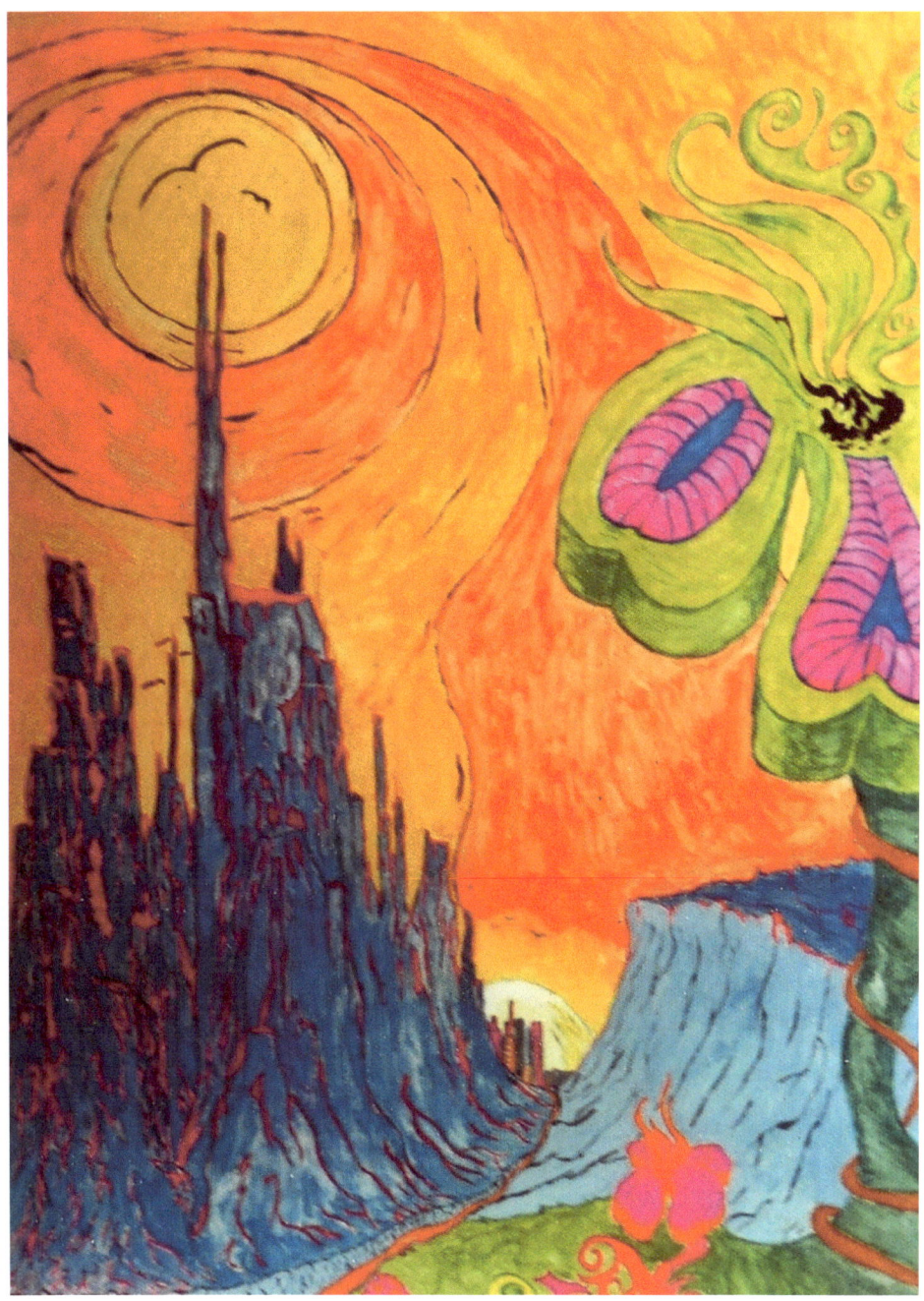

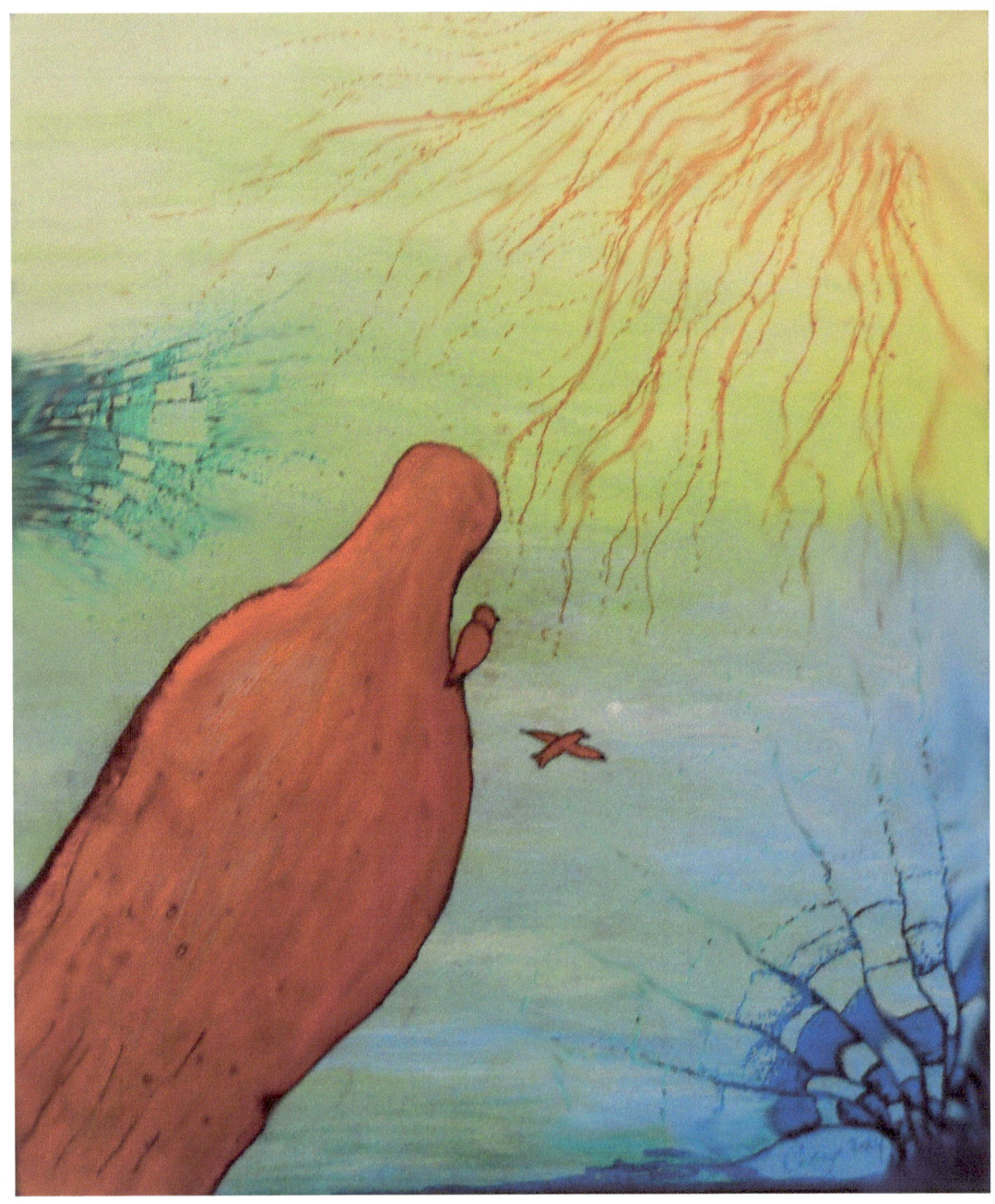

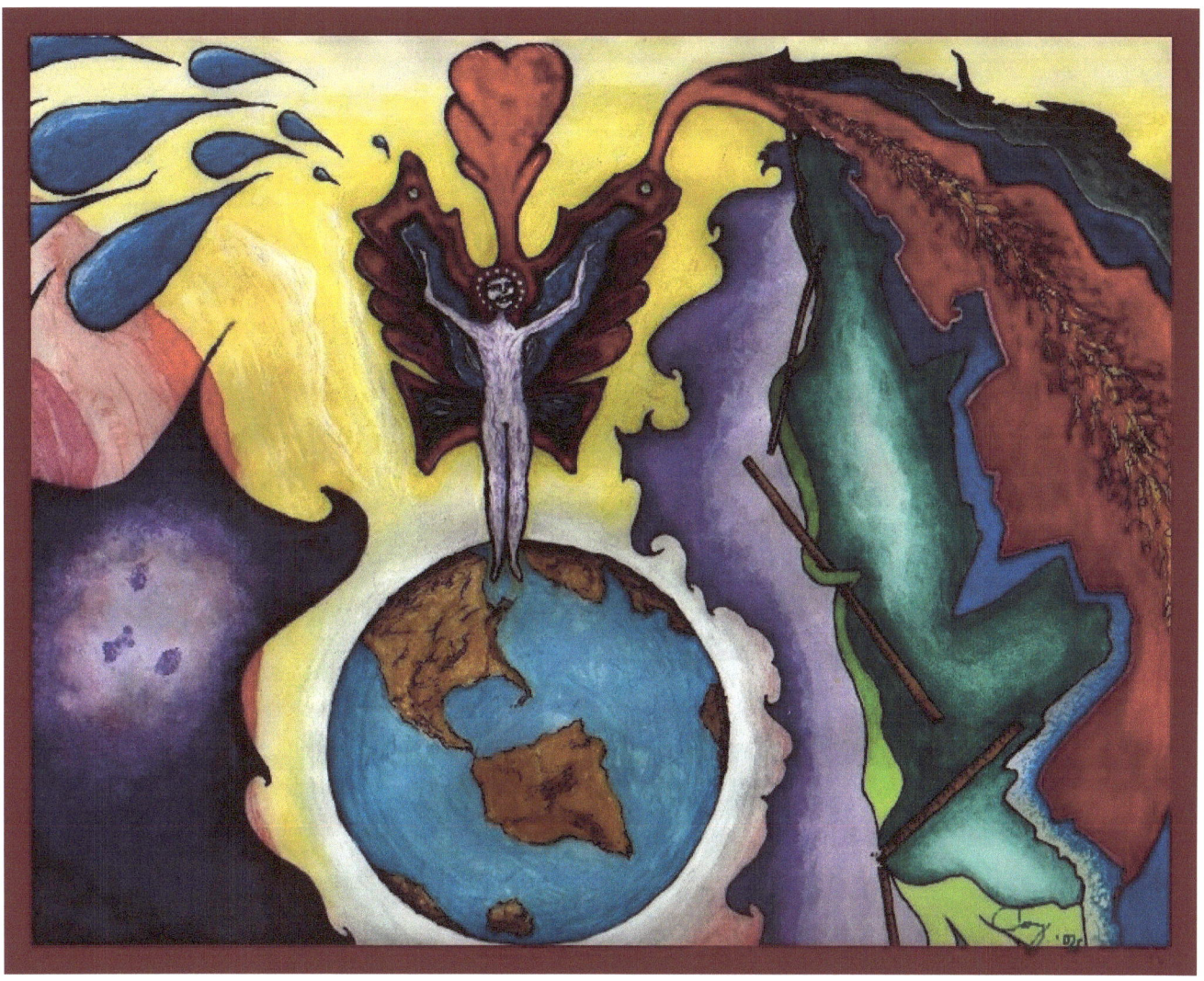

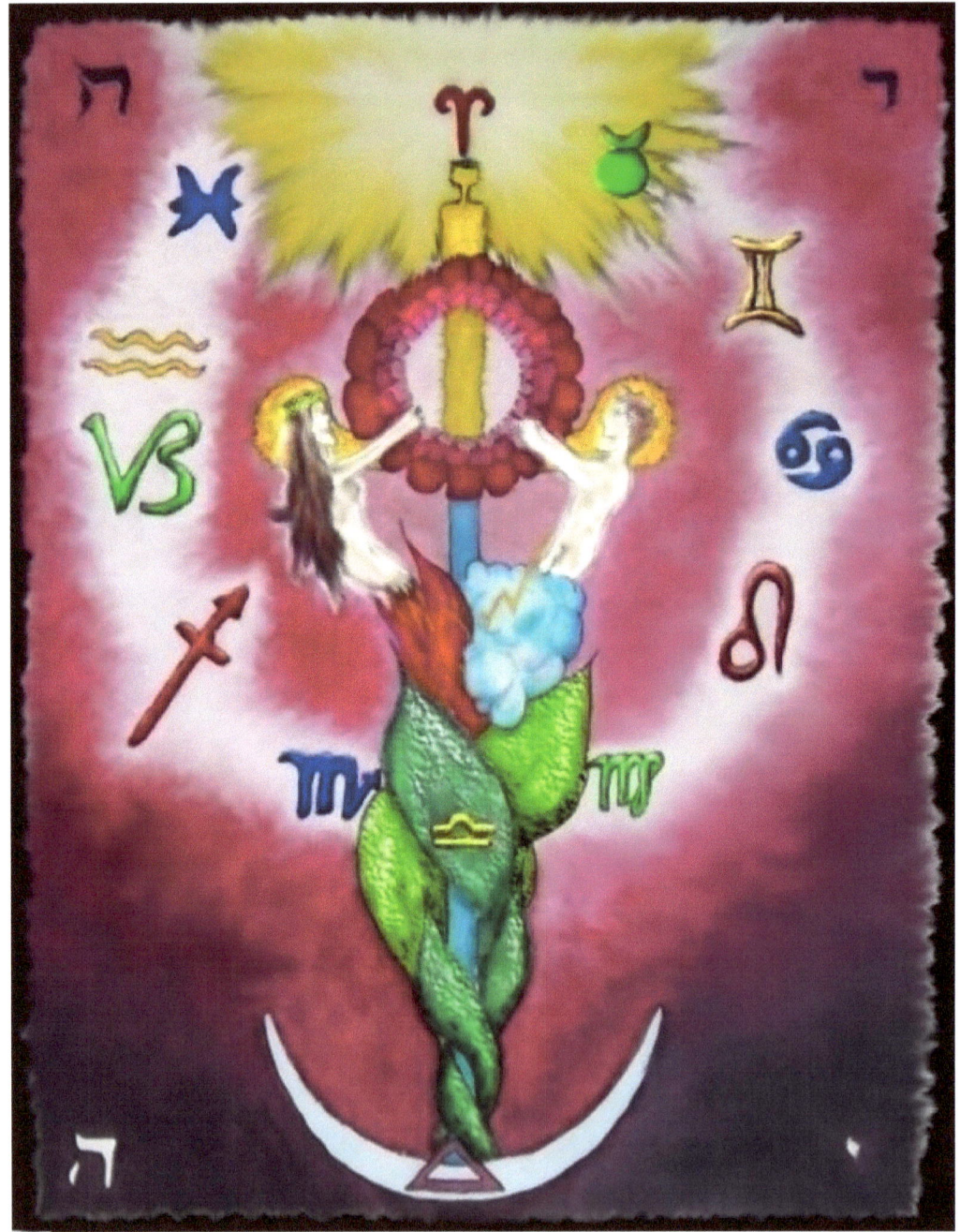

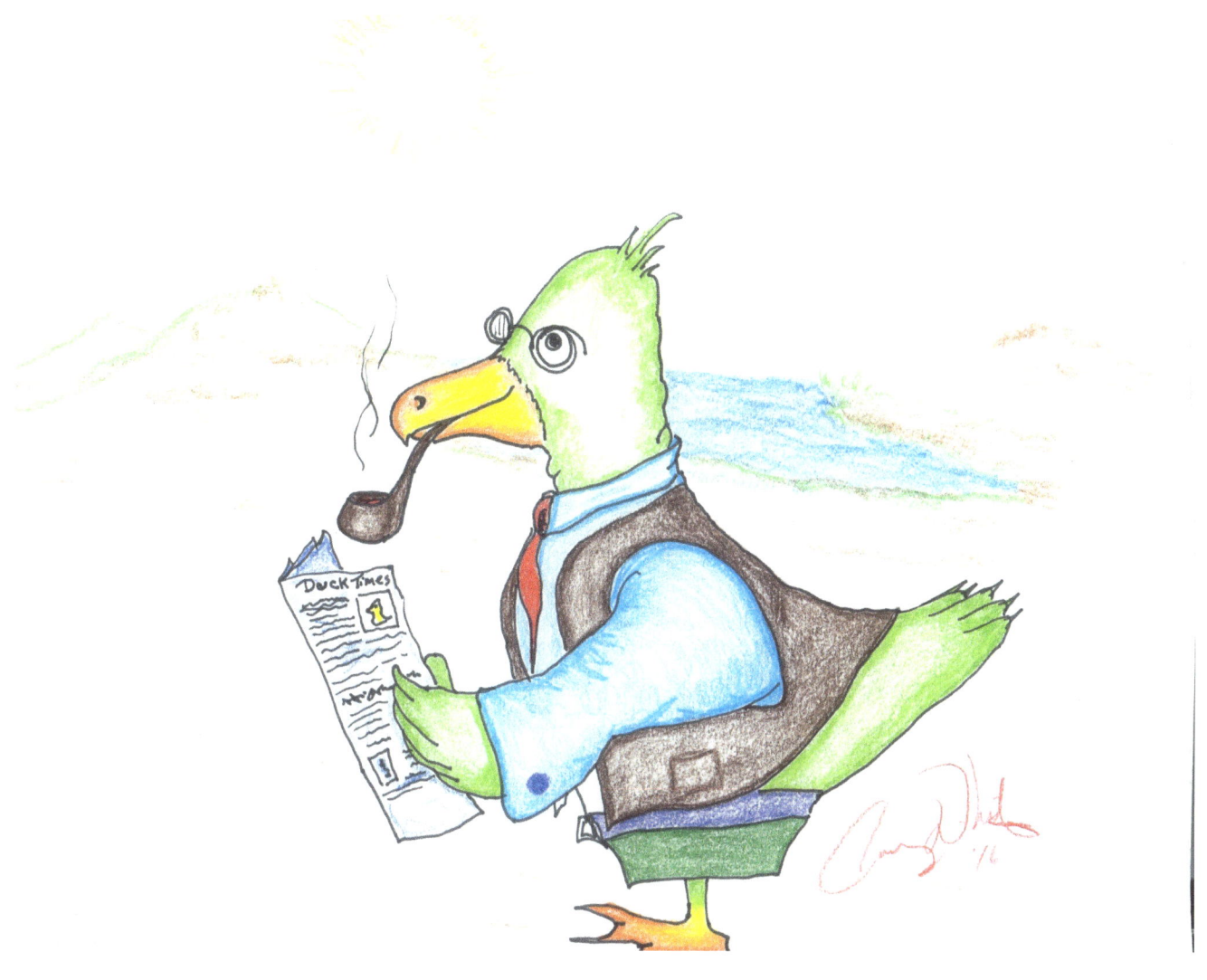

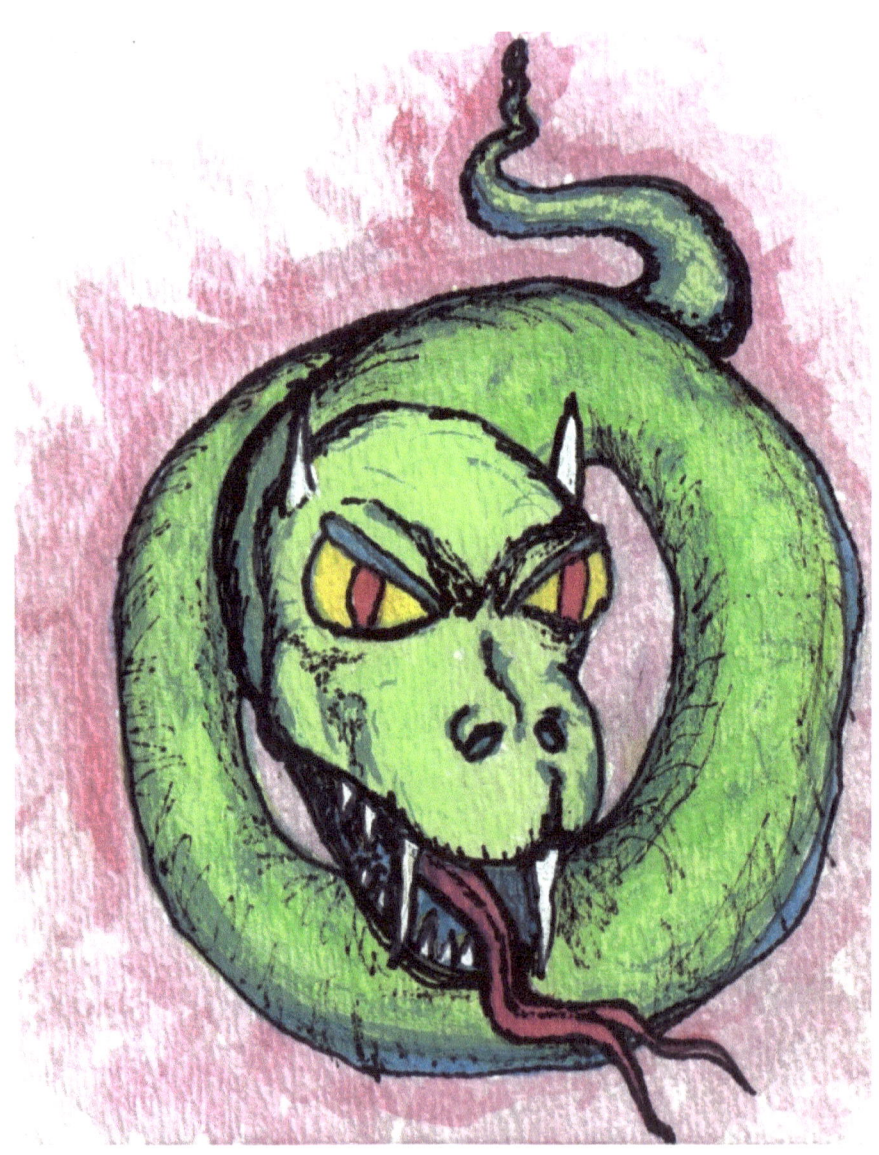

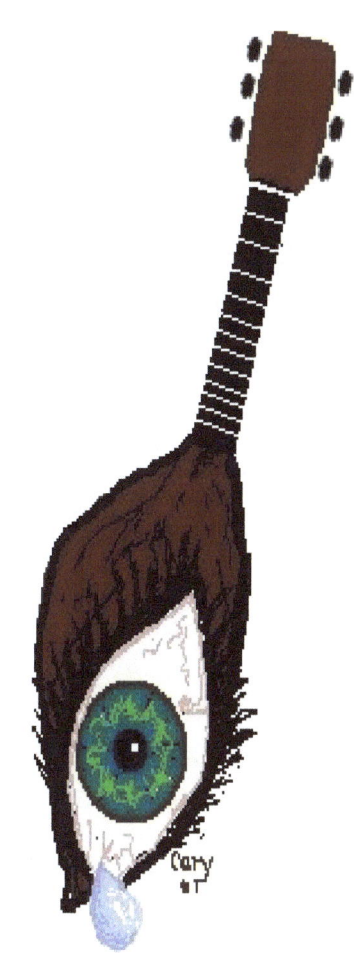

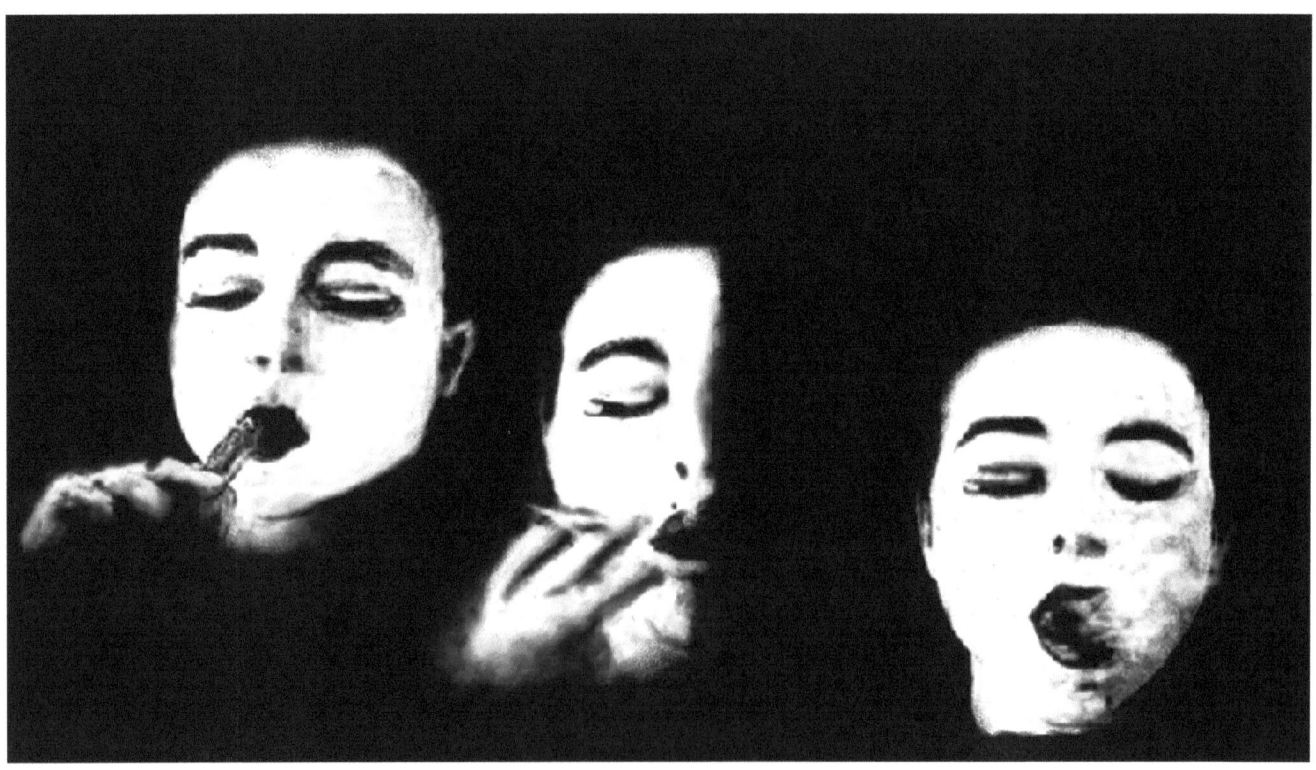

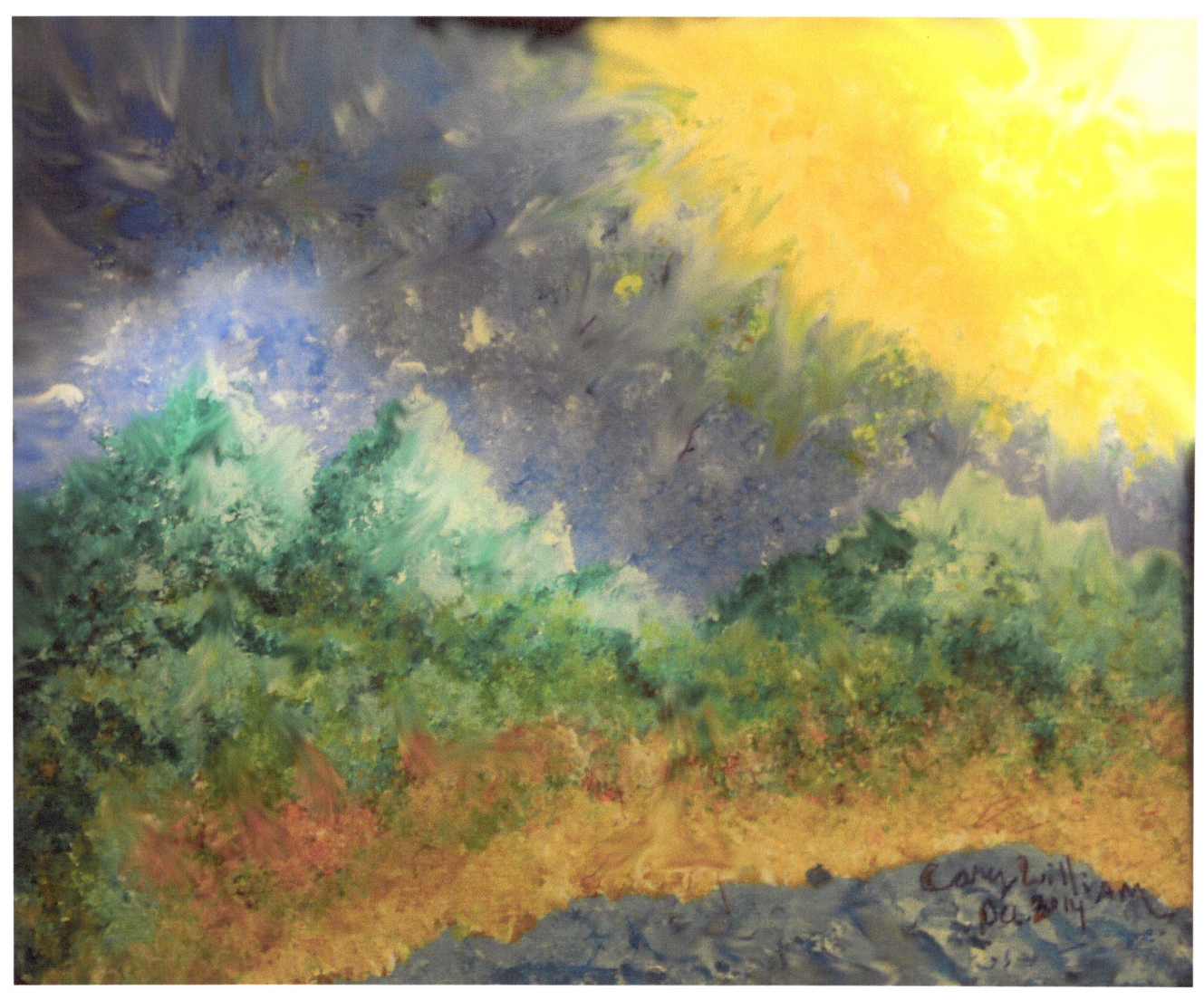

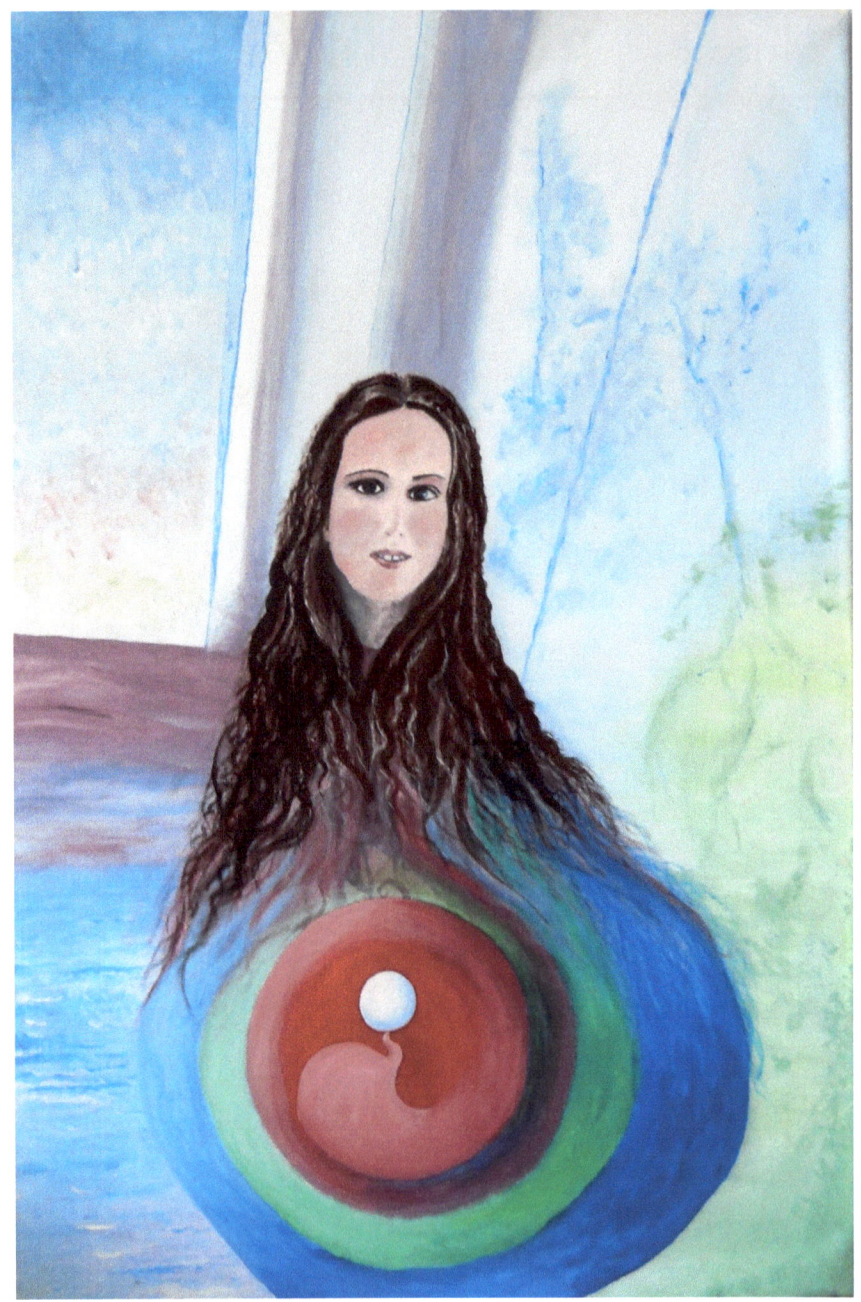

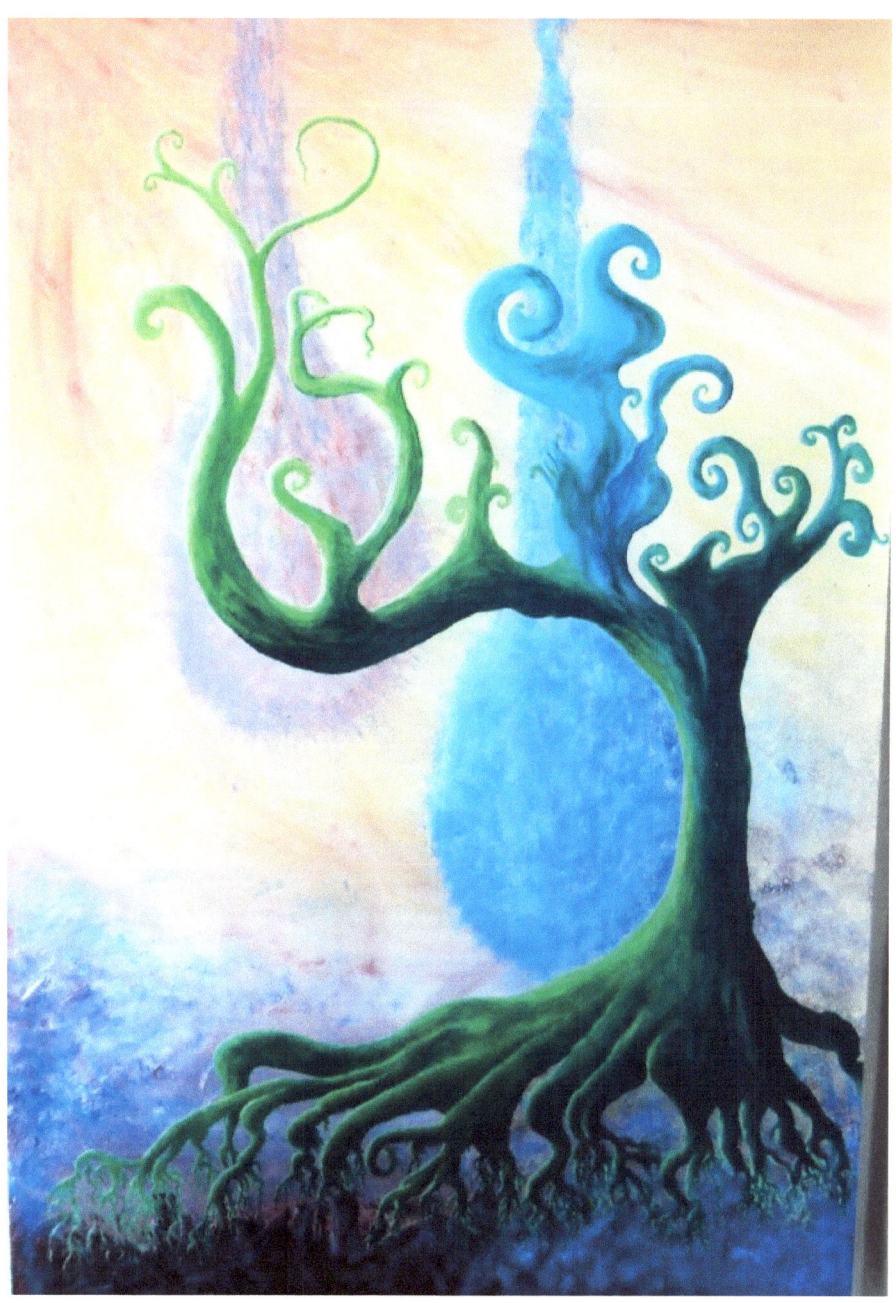

Cary William White

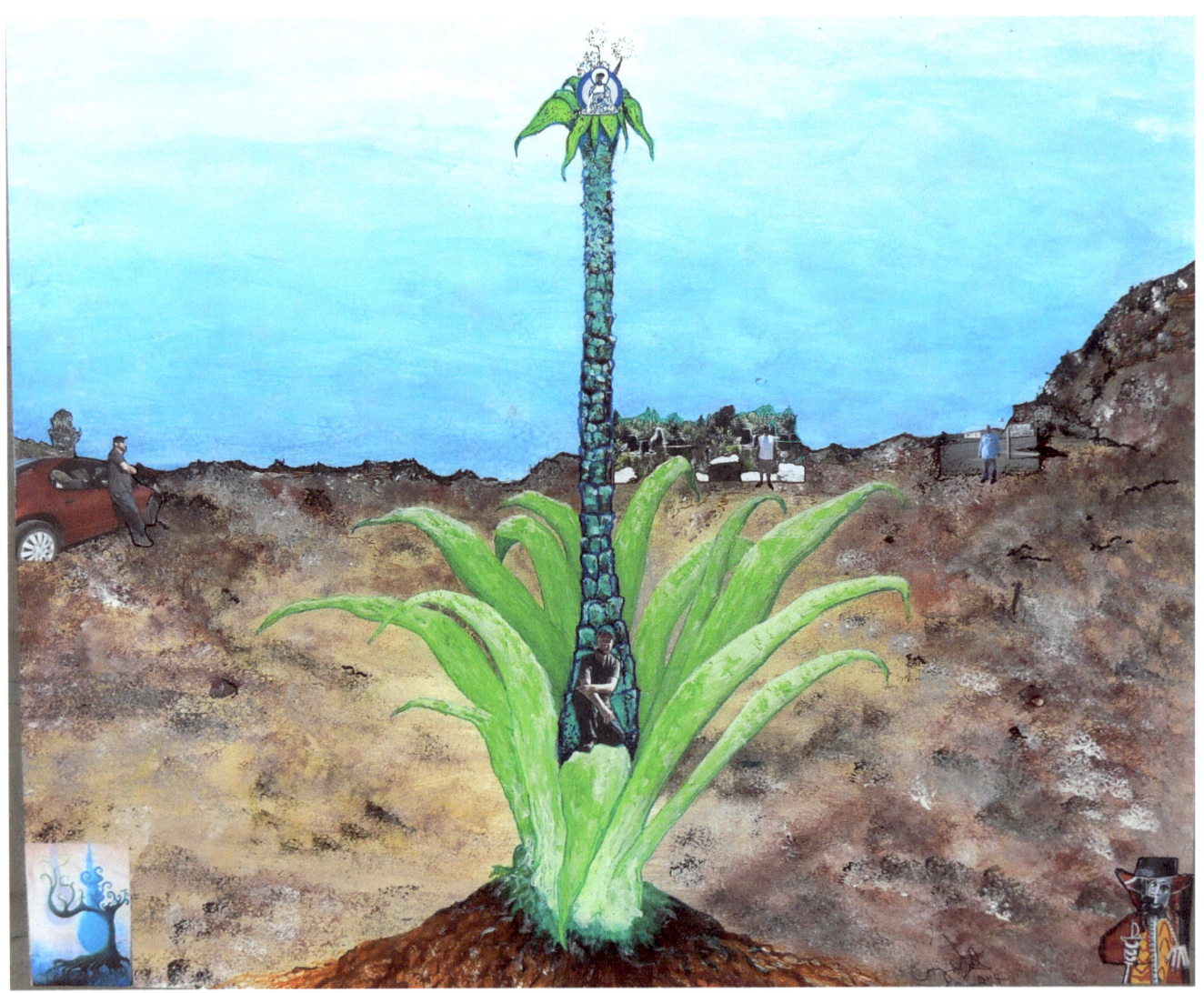

## III. WORLD'S BEYOND

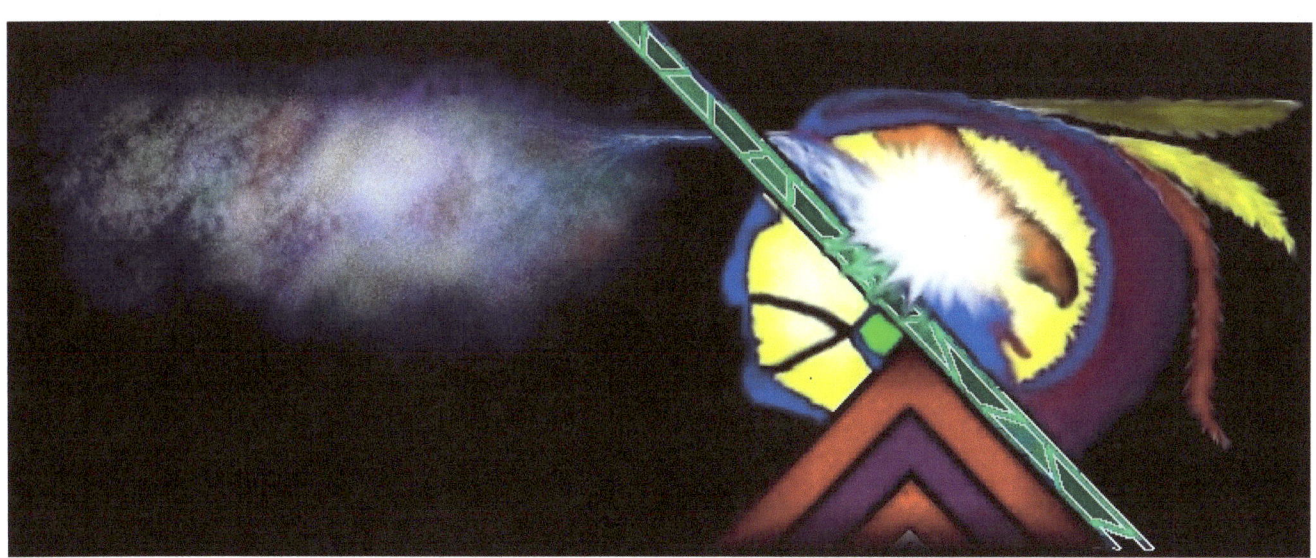

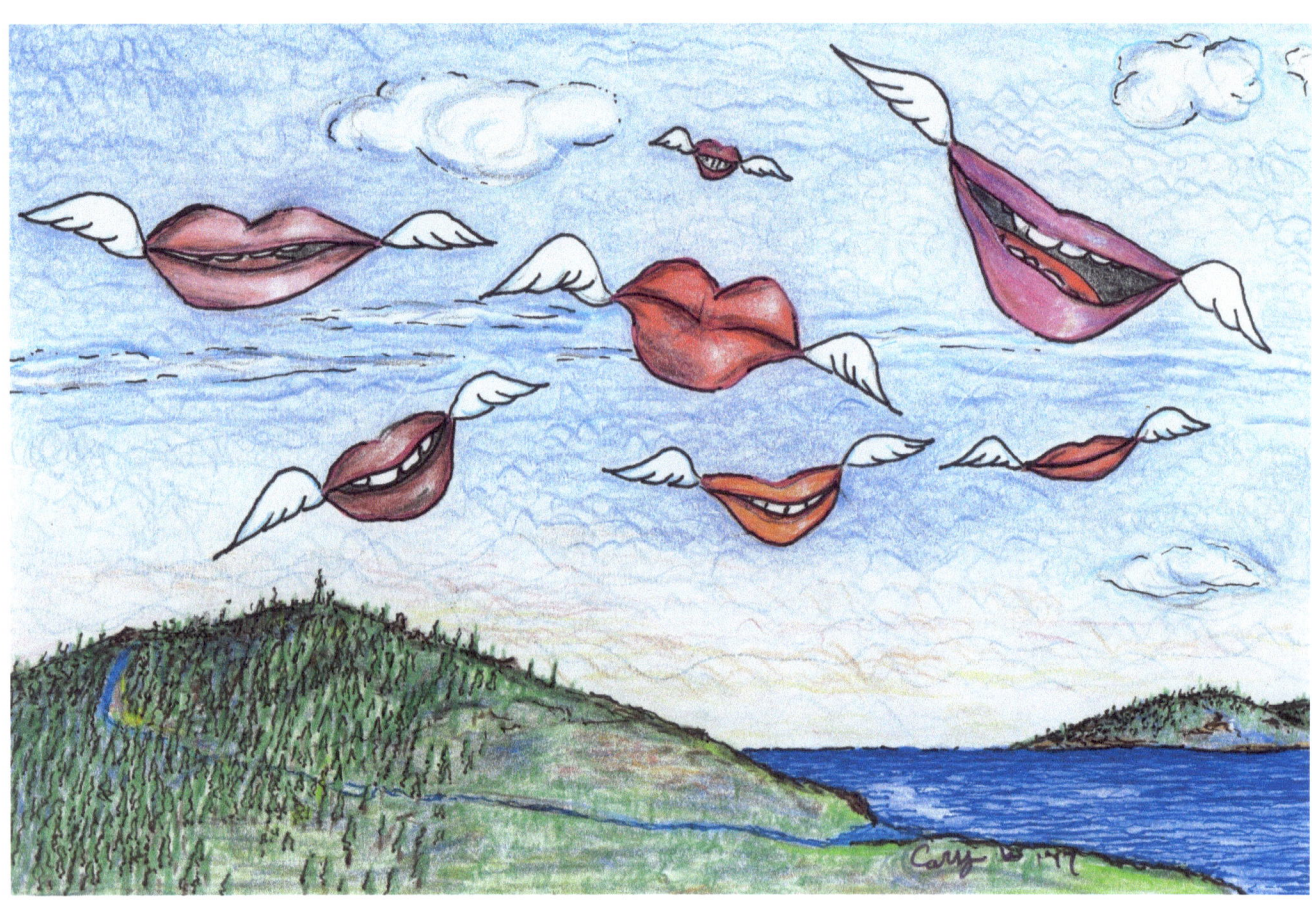

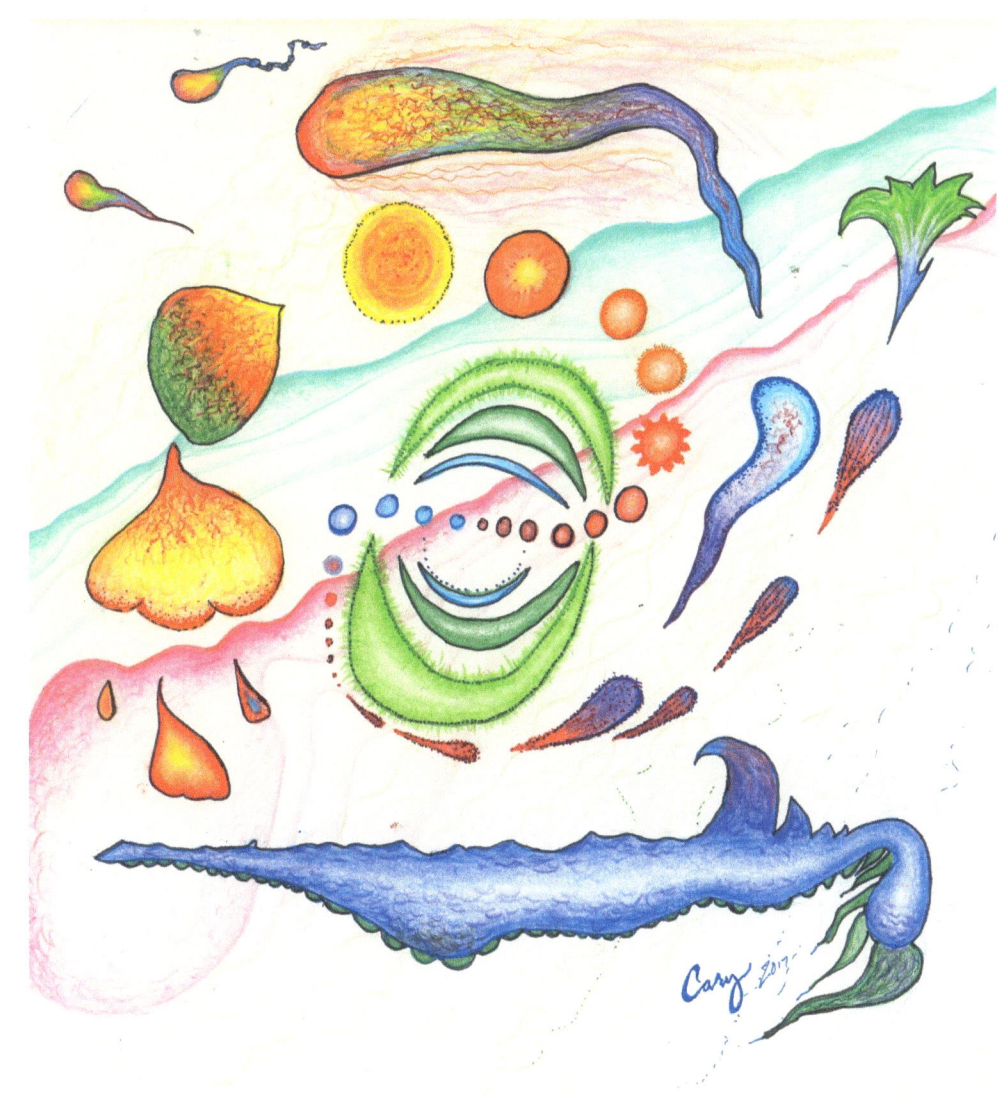

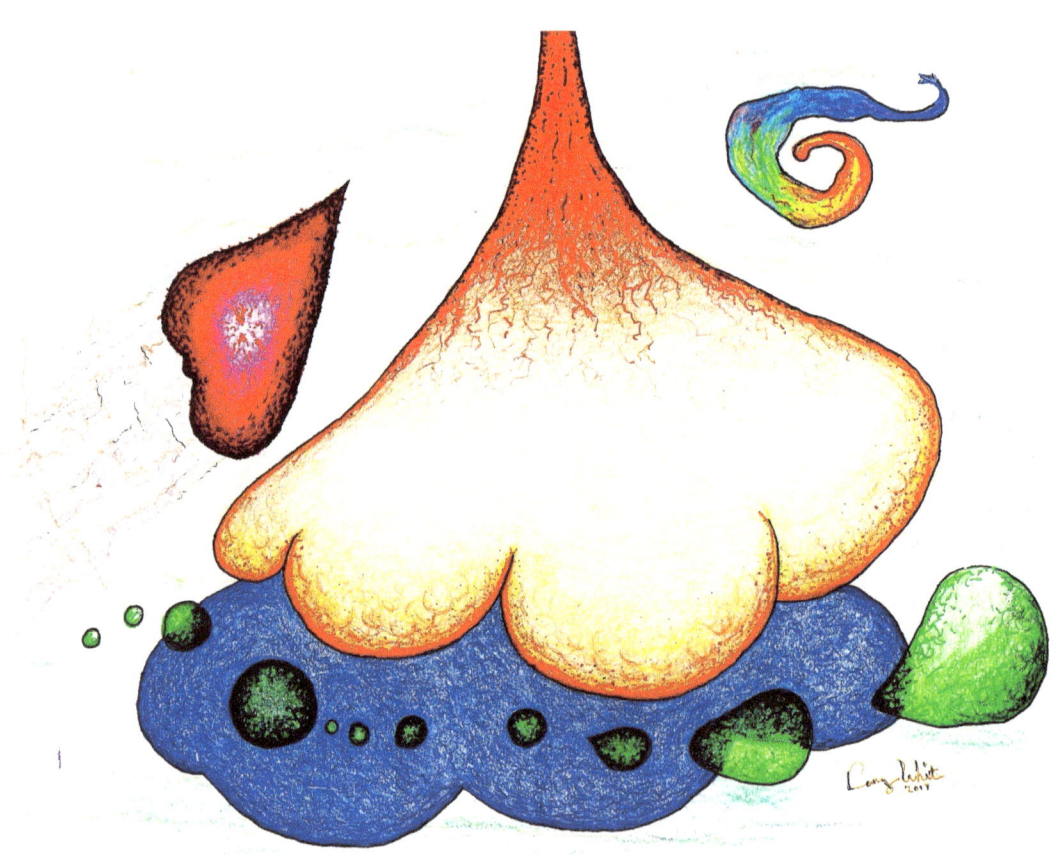

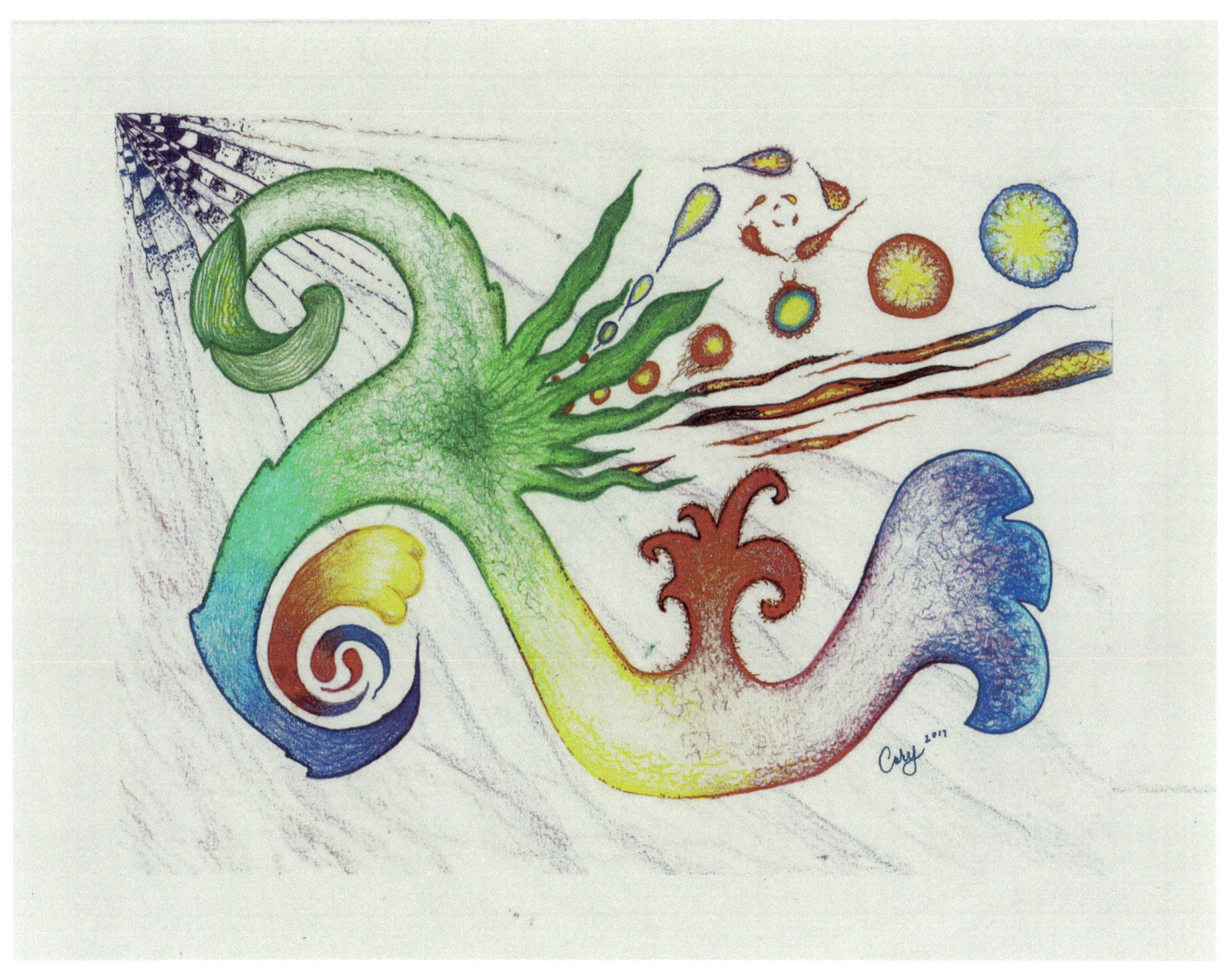

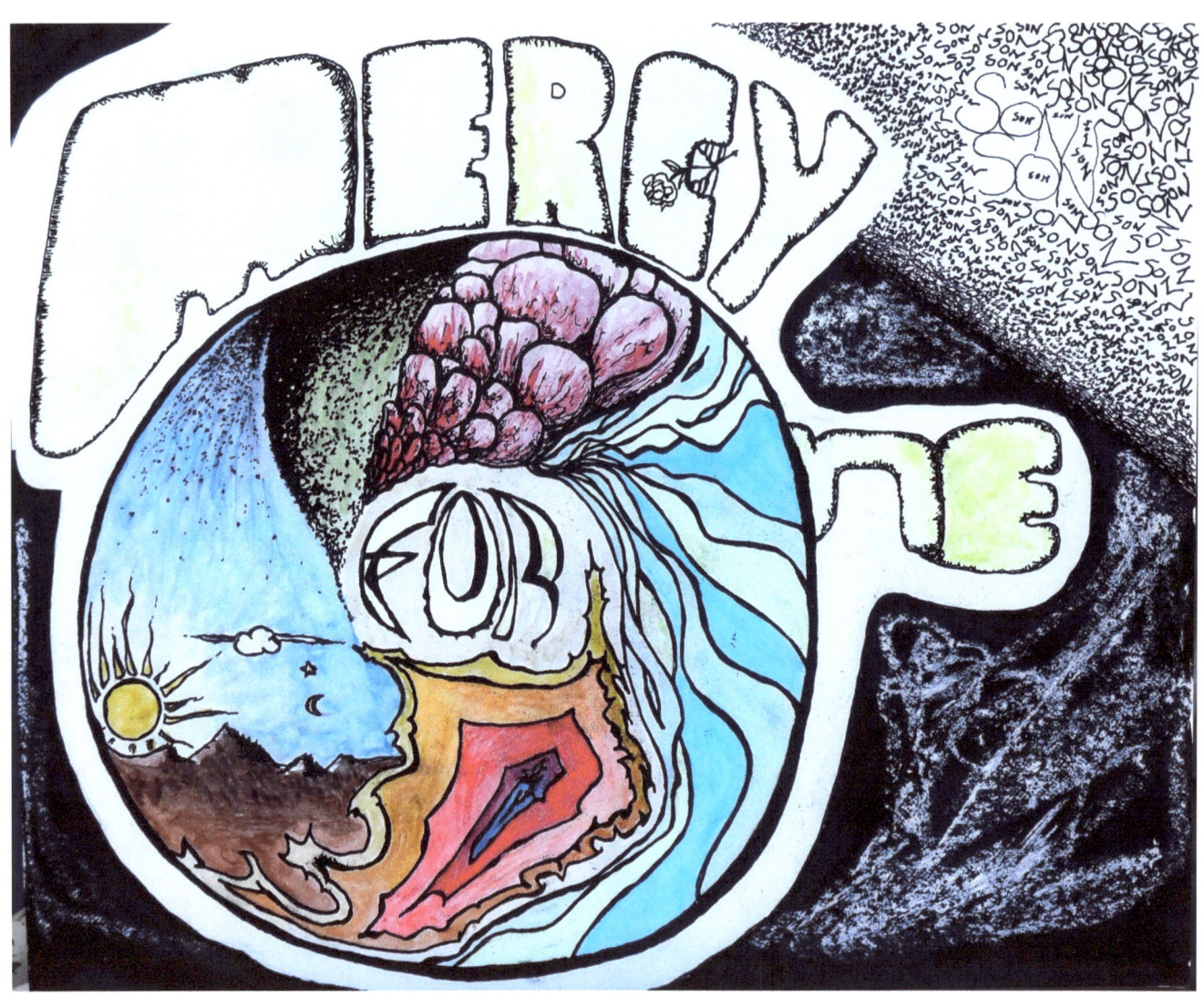

# DIMENSIONAL LENSES

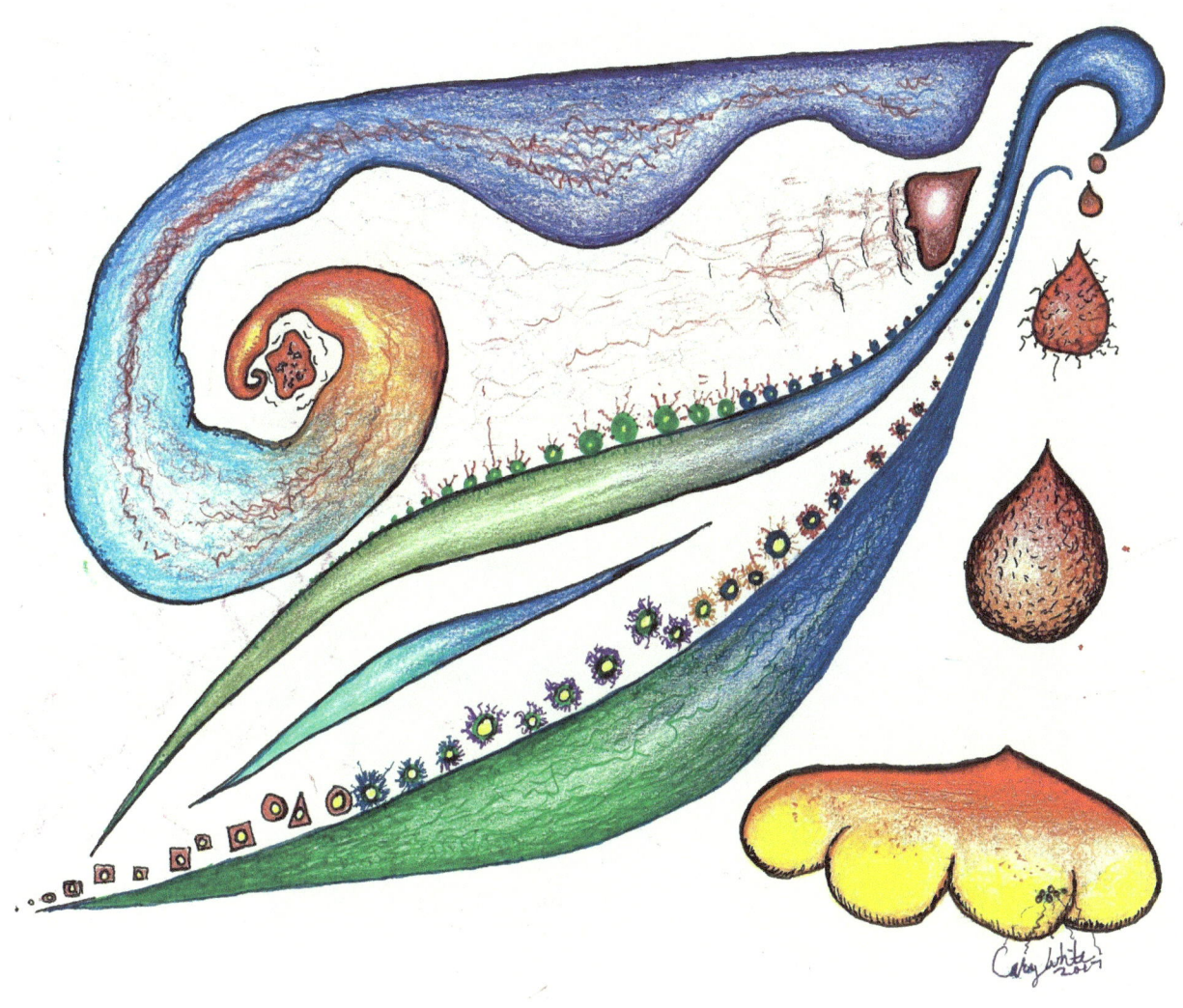

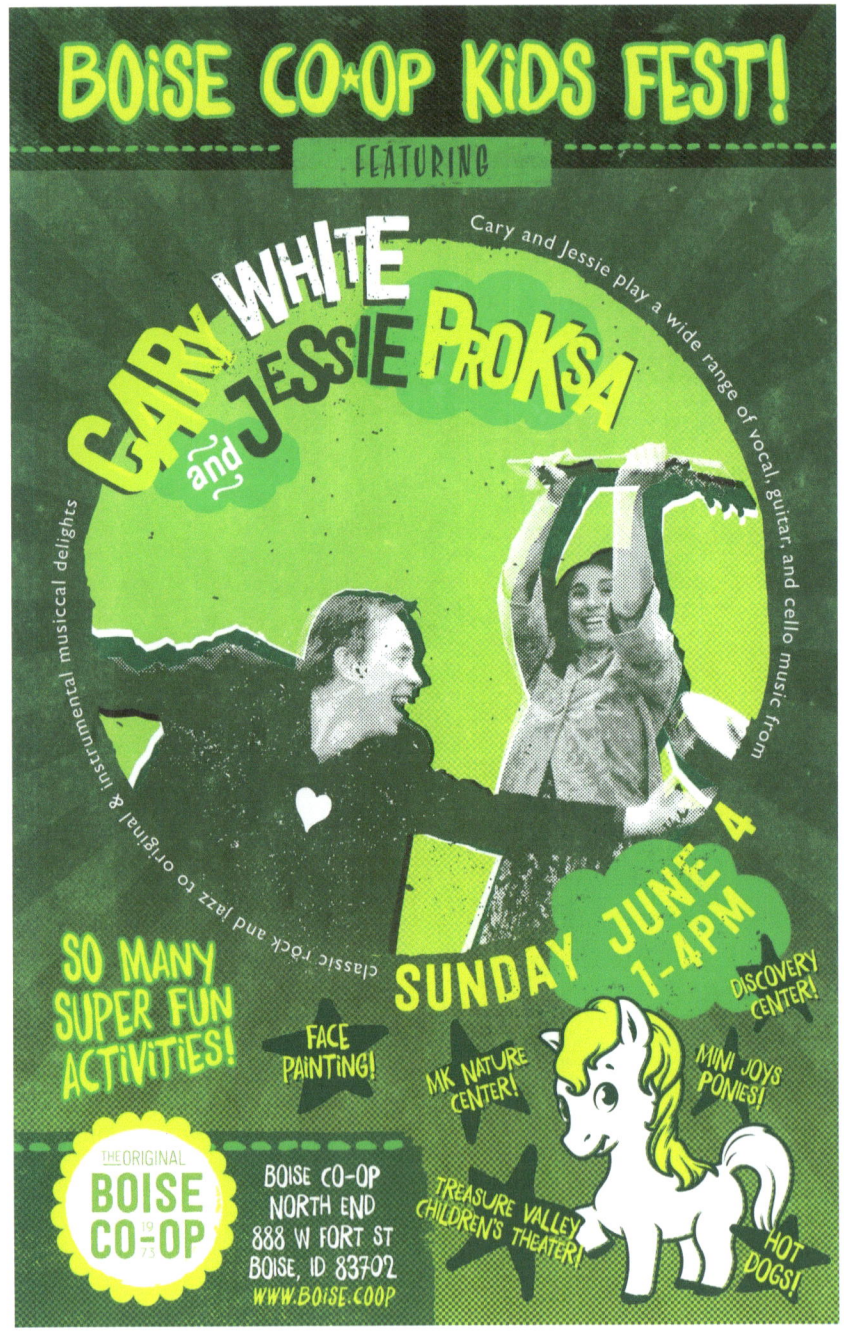

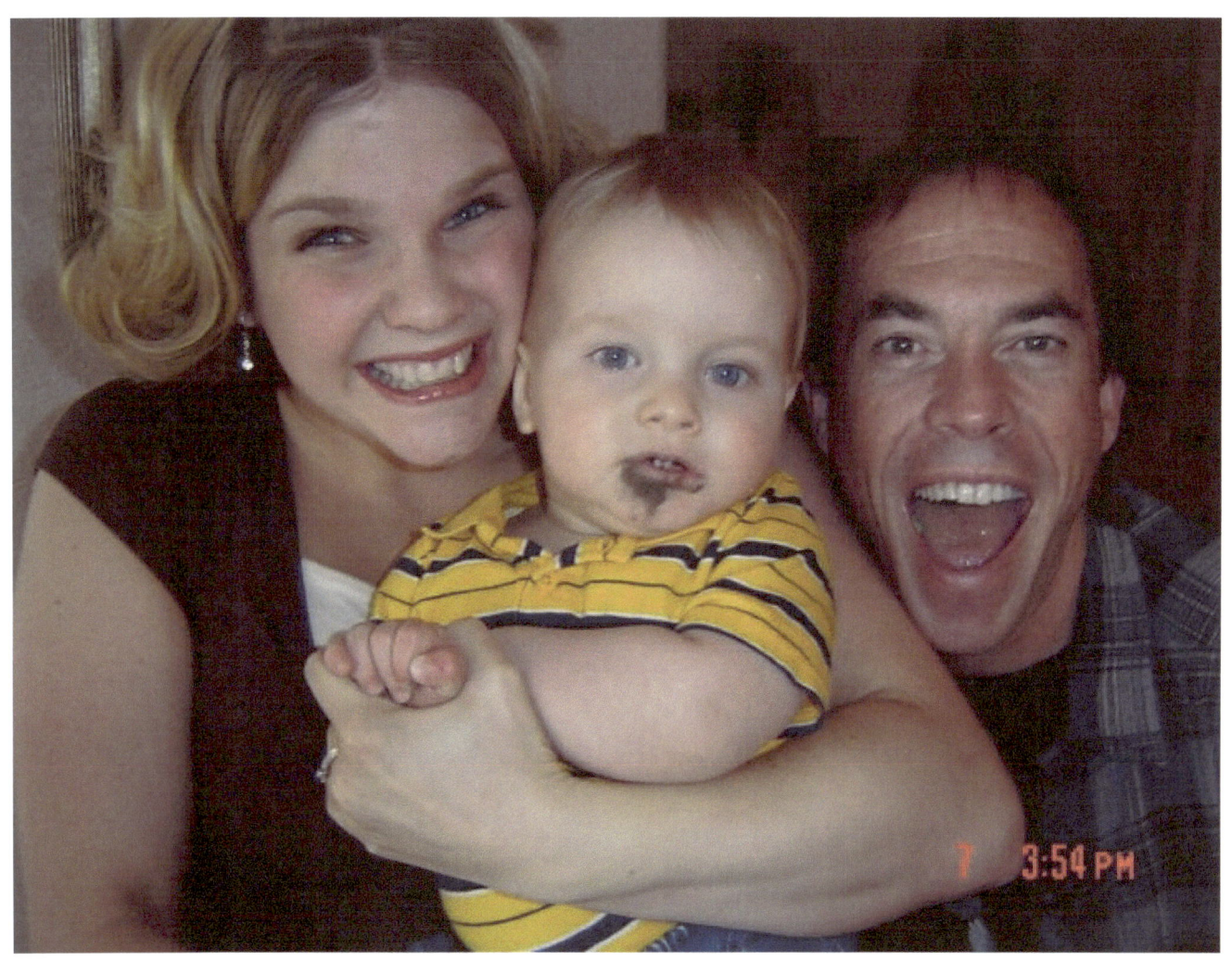

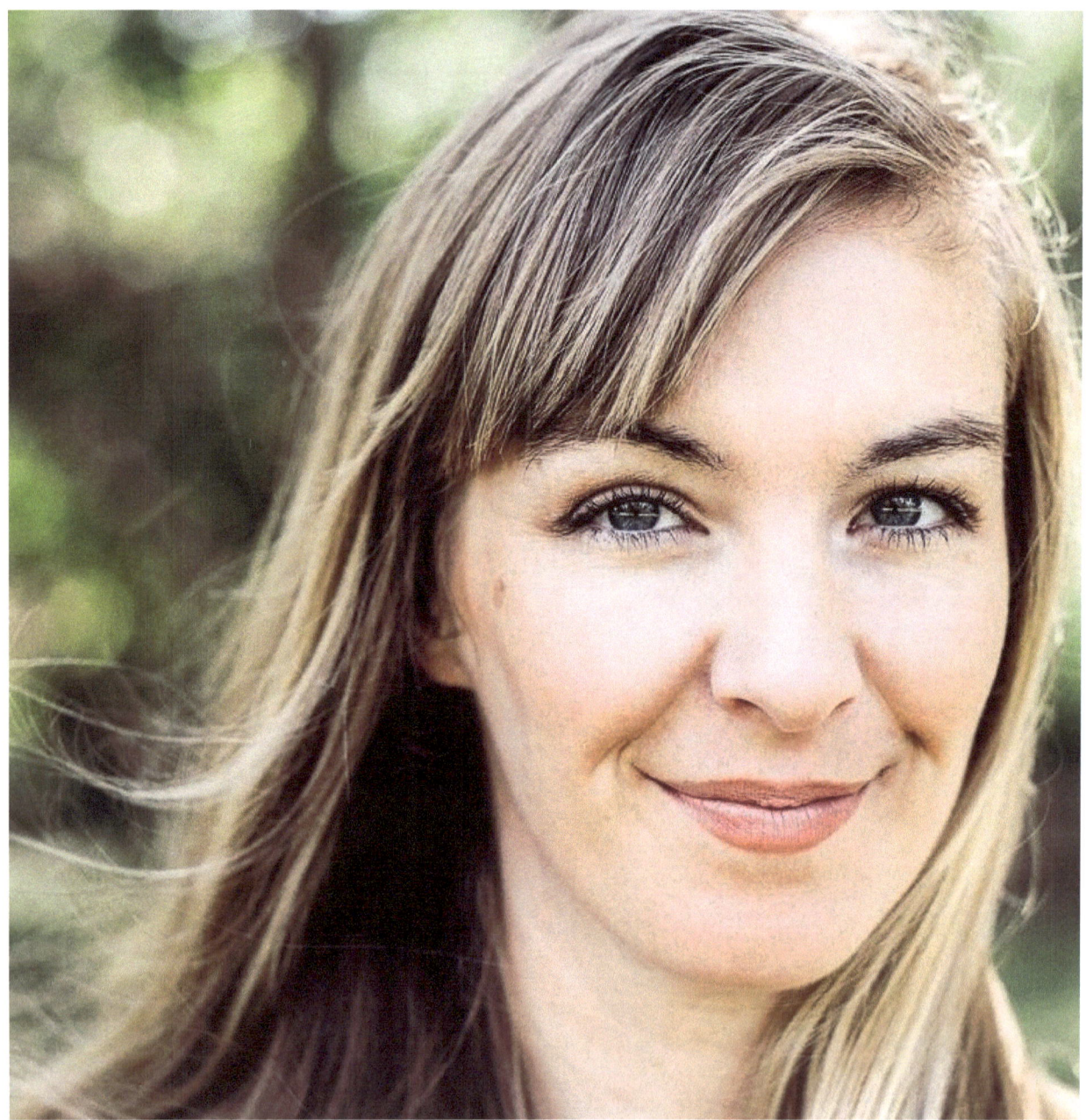

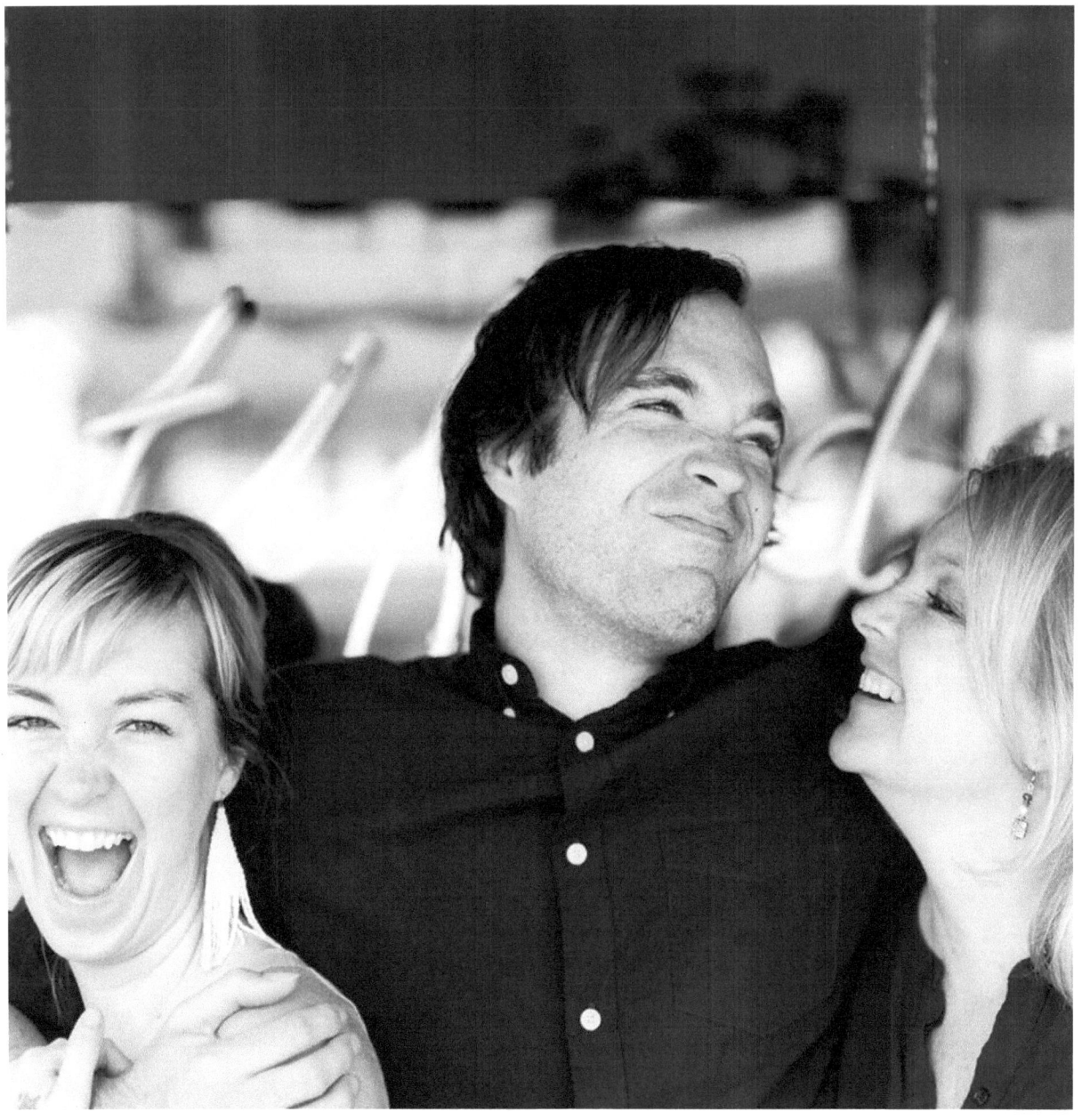

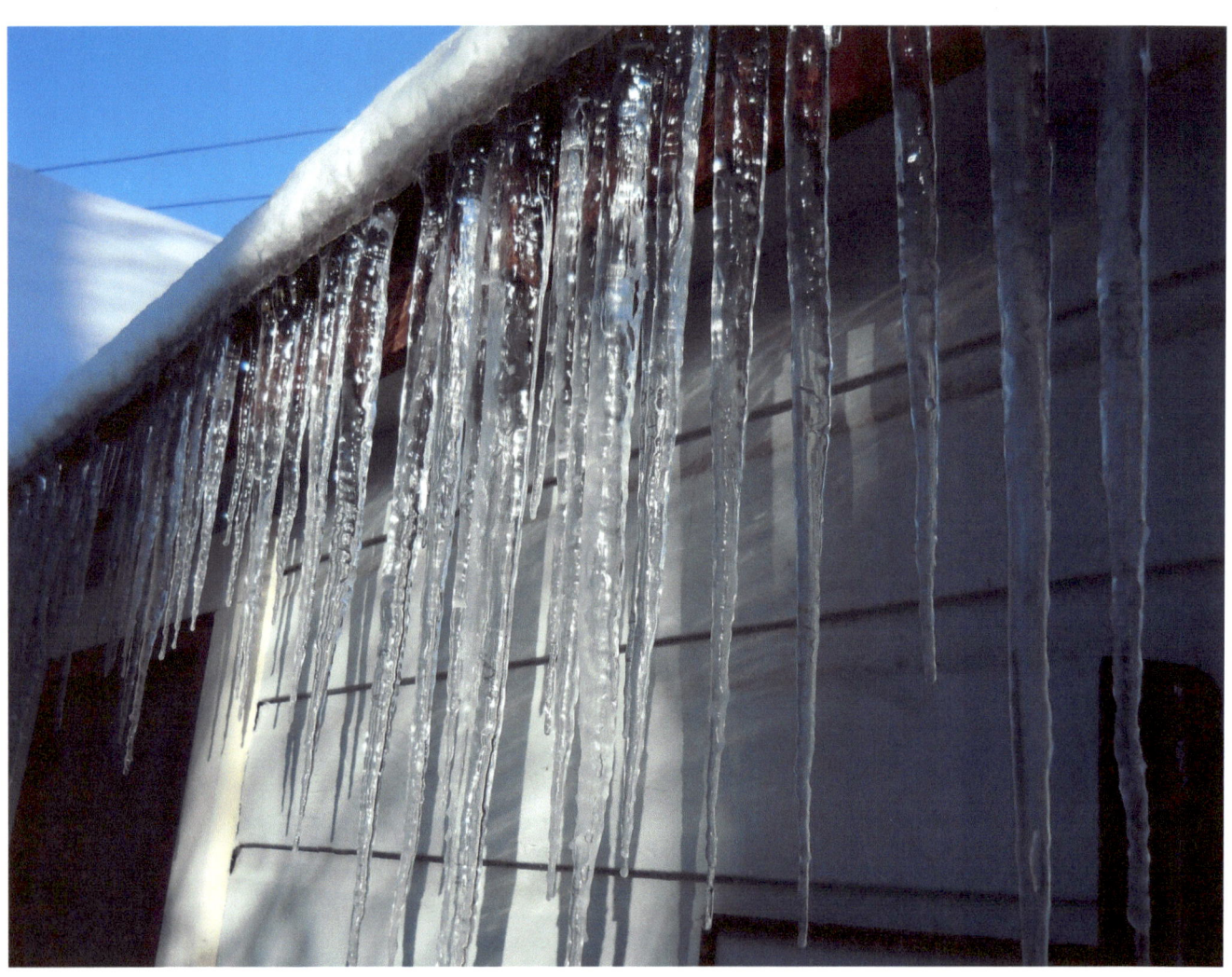

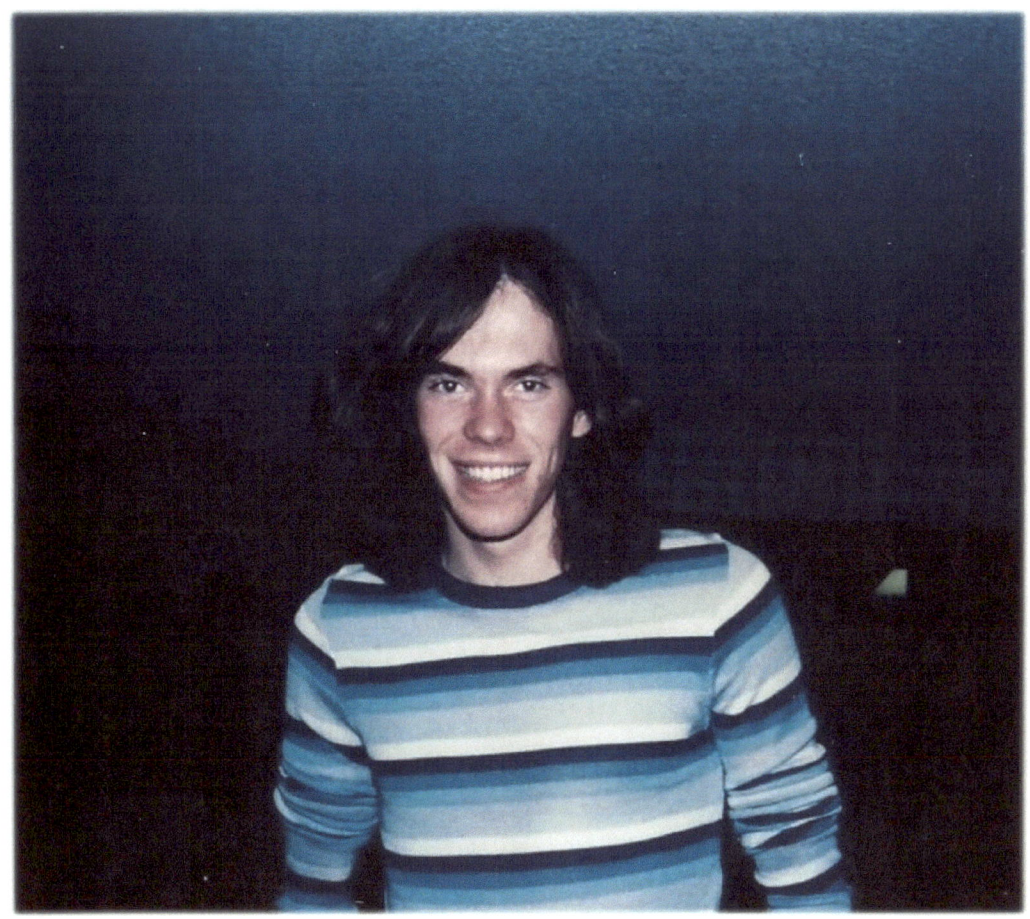

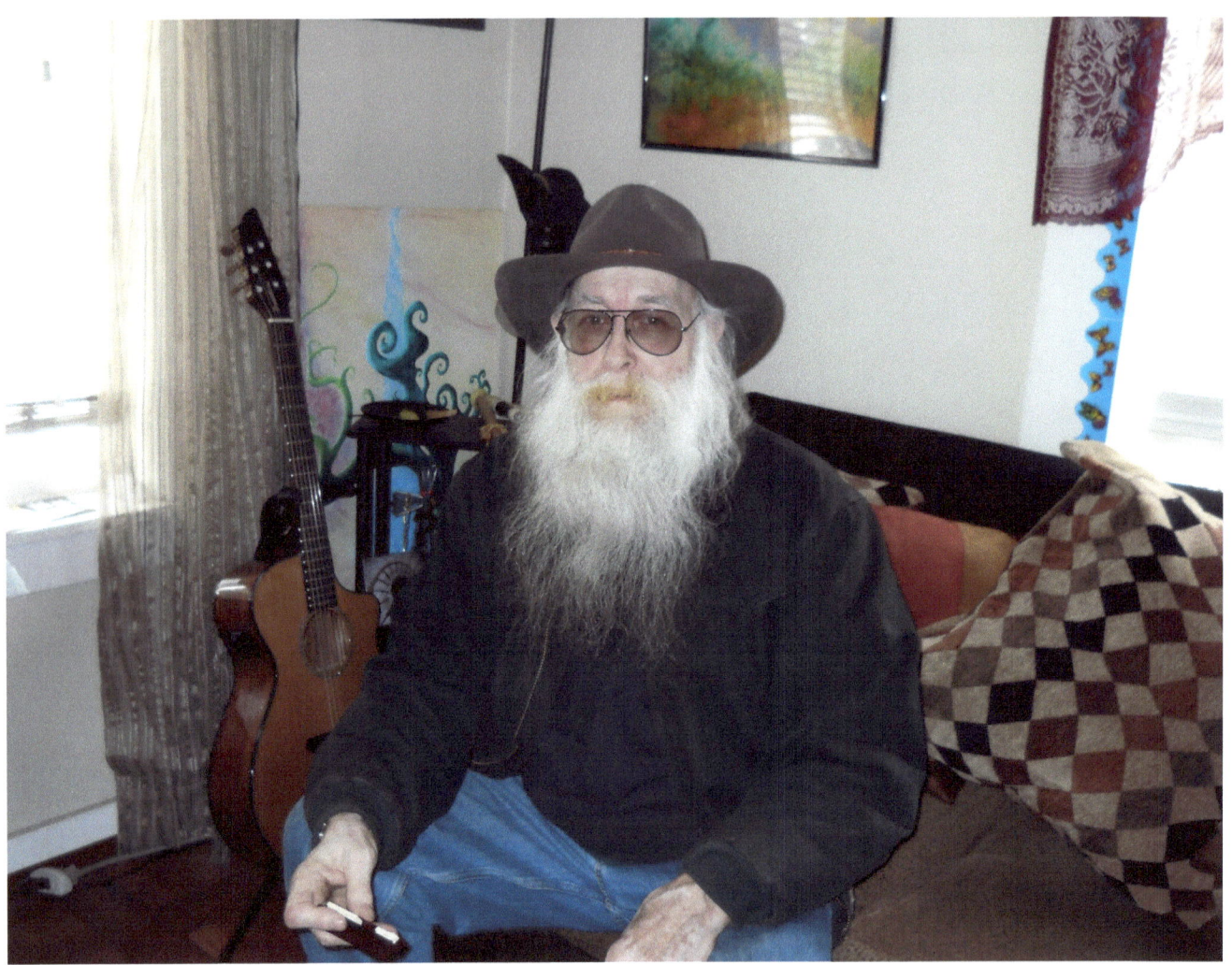

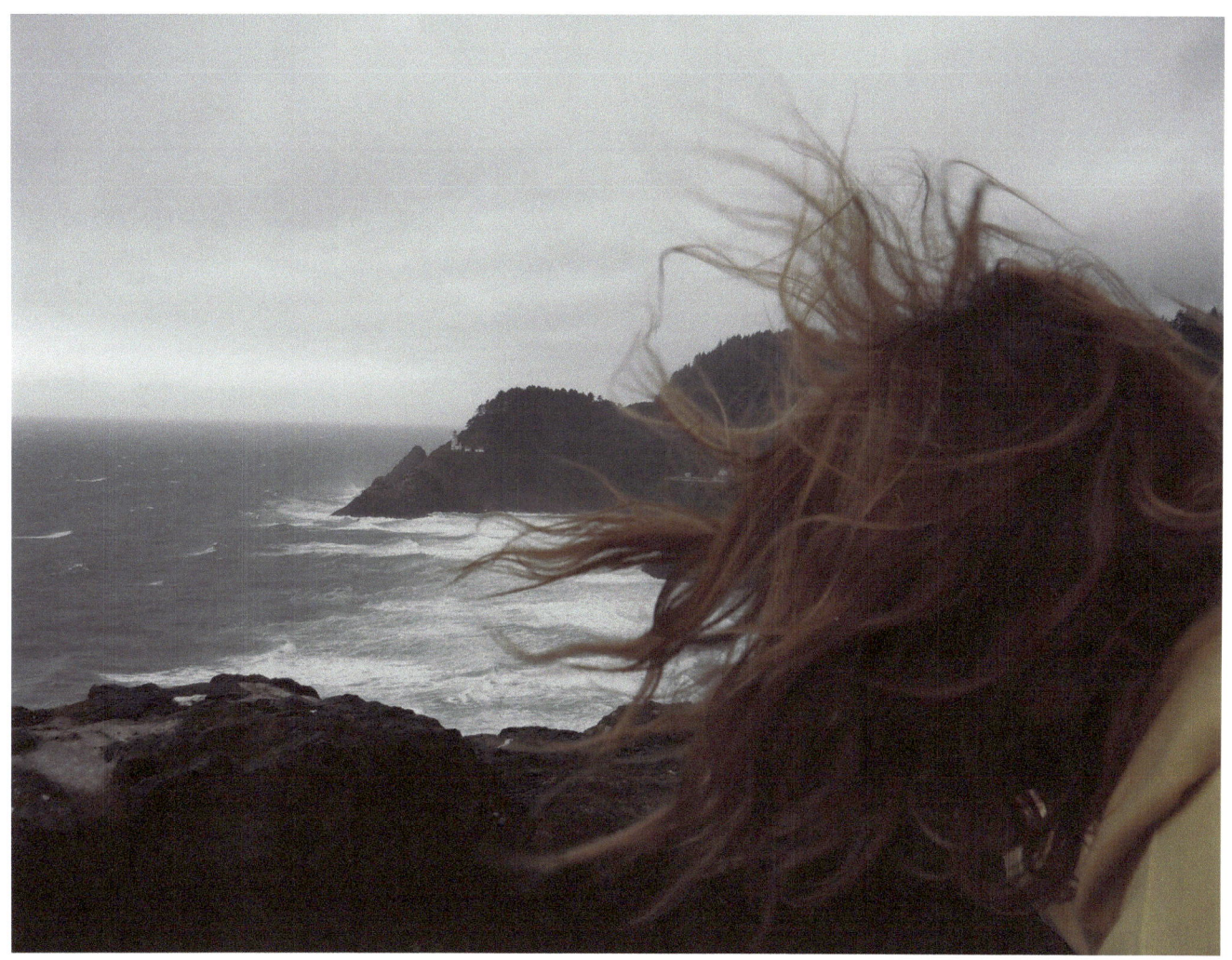

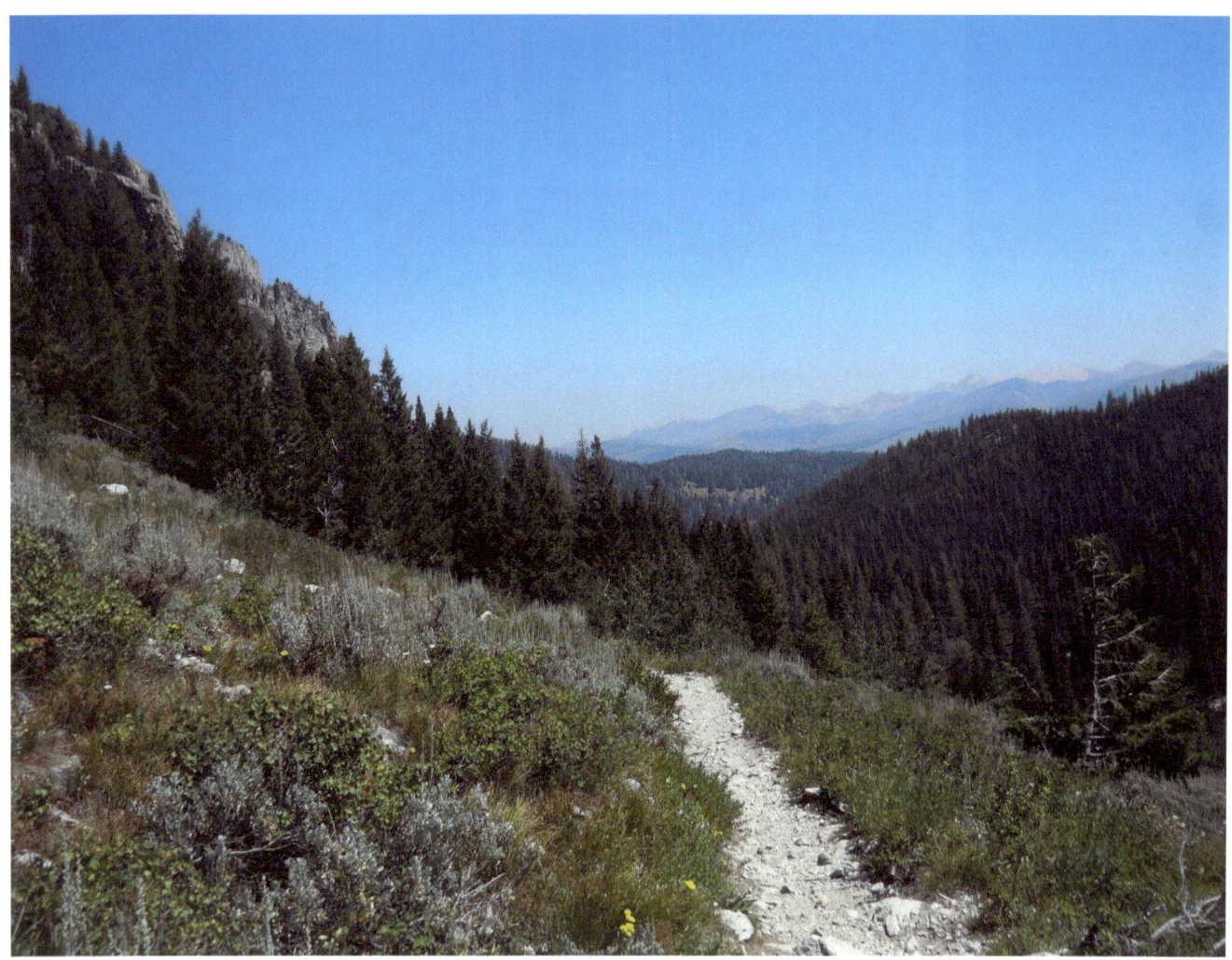

www.ingramcontent.com/pod-product-compliance
Lightning Source LLC
Chambersburg PA
CBHW042323250526
R18347300001B/R183473PG45473CBX00024B/23